Are You A
Spiritual Levite?

The Calling of the New Testament
Church Congregation

Donna M. Canada

WESTBOW
PRESS®
A DIVISION OF THOMAS NELSON
& ZONDERVAN

Scripture taken from the King James Version of the Bible.

Scripture taken from the Holy Bible, NEW INTERNATIONAL VERSION®. Copyright © 1973, 1978, 1984 by Biblica, Inc. All rights reserved worldwide. Used by permission. NEW INTERNATIONAL VERSION® and NIV® are registered trademarks of Biblica, Inc. Use of either trademark for the offering of goods or services requires the prior written consent of Biblica US, Inc.

WestBow Press books may be ordered through booksellers or by contacting:

WestBow Press
A Division of Thomas Nelson & Zondervan
1663 Liberty Drive
Bloomington, IN 47403
www.westbowpress.com
1 (866) 928-1240

ISBN: 978-1-5127-1906-2 (sc)
ISBN: 978-1-5127-1907-9 (e)

Library of Congress Control Number: 2015918533

Print information available on the last page.

WestBow Press rev. date: 11/14/2015

TABLE OF CONTENTS

ACKNOWLEDGEMENTS

Giving honor to God, Who is truly the Head of my life, I first want to express my deepest love, appreciation and thanksgiving to God for saving me and using me to write this book. My name may be on the cover as the author of the book, but my Lord Jesus Christ is the true Author. I was merely the scribe. The Lord is my life, my joy, my peace, my hope and the reason I live. Thank You, Lord Jesus, for loving me so and being ever so patient with me as You perfect me.

I sincerely thank my Bishop and Elect Lady, Prophet Phillip E. Owens, DD and Prophetess Patricia A. Owens, DD, who are the pastorate of my church, Immanuel's Temple Systems of Church and my spiritual parents. I could write a book --- and I may --- about how beautifully and holy you wear your Divine calling as God's prophets and shepherds of your congregational flocks. You have taught and led me, by precept and example, into a greater understanding of what it really means to be a Christian, how to live holy and how to serve the Lord in the beauty of holiness. I love and appreciate you so much. Through the inspiration of the Holy Ghost, you were the reason I was led to write this book. You are such jewels to be treasured by your local church congregations and the Church universal.

I give many thanks and hugs to my "little sis", Minister Rachel C. Owens, the principal of our church's K-12 Christian academy. You constantly encouraged me to write the book and you never let me give up on myself or the assurance that the book was the will of God. Timely conversations with you helped me to stay on track to write until God had completed what He wanted to say through the book. You truly are a "little lamb of love."

Thank you so much, my brother, Tom, for sending me a laptop to use when my computer crashed and I had no funds to buy another one. You enabled me to continue working on the manuscript, despite the attempts of the enemy to hinder me. Just by doing that, you drove the spirit of discouragement away from me.

I thank my spiritual daughter, Latisha, for always telling me, "Mom, you can do this." I thank you for reading some of my writings before they became "a book" and telling me how they blessed you. You were such a cheerleader for me. Hug yourself for me, my Tisha. You are my special gift from God.

Finally, I thank my best friend and prayer partner of 25 years and counting, my real spiritual "sister in Christ", Yvonne. Proverbs 17:17 says: *"A friend loveth at all times…"* (King James Version), and 1 Corinthians 13: 8 says: *"Charity [love] never faileth…."* "Vonn", you have never, ever failed to be a true friend and sister to me, from the first day we met after I had soon joined our church. We have been through so much together as we entered the process of being perfected by God for His service -- laughing, crying, praying, praising, worshiping, wondering, agreeing and disagreeing. But always, we kept upholding each other and our leaders, as we kept our eyes on Jesus, and He upheld us both. So many times in our conversations and our work in the house of the Lord the Holy Ghost has been right in the midst of us. I could not have begun or finished this book without your support, my Sis. Love ya!

INTRODUCTION

Thank you for opening this book. I pray it will be a blessing to you. Before you read further, let me clarify that this book is not for those who are looking for an intellectual course in Christianity 101. Nor is it a book for those who are merely contemplating becoming a Christian sometime in the distant future. And it is not a book for those who are just *curious* about what this Christianity "stuff" is all about.

This book addresses a very specific audience. The audience includes those who are fairly new Christians, "baby saints". The audience includes those who have been saved for many years, "seasoned saints". The audience includes those who have committed themselves to a life of holiness and obedience to the commandments of God. This book is for those who have obeyed God by assembling themselves with other believers, as members of a **God-ordained**, **Bible-based** church, headed by a **God-appointed** leader. This book is for the congregation.

So many books have been written and so many opinions given about the responsibilities a pastor owes to his church and congregation. So many members of the laity have opinions about what a pastor is supposed to do or not do for his congregation, and what it takes to be a good pastor. But have you ever engaged in a discussion or even asked yourself what your responsibility is as a member of the congregation? Have you ever asked yourself what your responsibilities are to your spiritual leaders? While you were critiquing this or that pastor and first lady, did you ever stop to critique yourself, congregation member?

Perhaps some of you were members of a church whose pastor or first lady fell from grace, or left the ministry and church due to exhaustion or disgust. Now, while you were pointing fingers at them, "tsk-tsking" and wondering how they could have "abandoned" you, did you ever ask if *you* had done all *you* could have to prevent this tragedy from happening? Did you ever wonder if you were the reason they left the ministry in disgust, frustration, or with a feeling of failure? I'm just asking.

On the other hand, some of you are blessed to have God-chosen pastors who have not fallen from grace or worn themselves out. Some of you have leaders who are still on the battlefield for the Lord, still holding high the banner of HOLINESS as well as living it. Praise God for that; it is a great blessing. But are you doing what you need to do to ensure that your pastor and first lady do not fall victim to the wiles and snares of the devil? Are you doing what you need to do to guard their backs while they watch for your souls? Some of you have already quickly answered with a resounding "YES!" without giving it much thought. After all, you do volunteer to serve on some church committee or auxiliary.

BUT

- Is mere membership on an auxiliary all that is necessary?
- Does God only expect you to have your "name on the roll" as a member of the congregation, with a member number for the offering envelope?
- Is there more you should be doing?
- Is there more you should *be*?
- Does God require more of you?
- Are you performing your duties in the church as God says you should?
- Are you serving with the right attitude and for the right reasons?
- Do you know the Biblical reason you are suppose to work in the church?
- Are you a help or a hindrance to your pastor?
- Are you a joy or grief to your pastor and first lady?
- Is your service a sweet savor offered up to God, or merely an empty activity and a foul smell in the nostrils of God?

I'm just asking.

This book is for the *members* of the church congregation to consider their roles and responsibilities to their pastor, as members of the congregation. The focus is on the flock your pastor has been commanded to lead. The focus is on the individuals whose souls have been given to your pastor to shepherd and keep safe along this Christian journey. This book is for those in the church who have a mind and heart's desire to work *with* their pastor and not *against* their pastor. If this is you, you need to read this book. Pray that God speaks to you as you read it. Don't rush to give this book to your pastor or first lady to read. You read it yourself. This one's for you!

God-chosen, God-ordained pastors are such a gift and treasure to their congregations. I'm talking about the pastors who are truly submitted to God and who sincerely live a life of holiness before God and man, in obedience to the word and commands of God, not according to the designs and dictates of self. It is time that we, as the congregation, start being to them what the word of God foreshadowed us to be to them—spiritual Levites, the first *helps ministries* to God's chosen leaders. Even though the duties and purpose of the Levites were spelled out in the Old Testament, I believe the *spirit* of the command to the Levitical order can be applied to New Testament Christian congregations as we follow our leaders.

And that is what this little book is all about. Members, let's put the examination light on ourselves and see what we discover. May God bless, help, deliver, convert and anoint us to do our Christian duty to God and to our pastors.

(*DISCLAIMER*: Throughout this book my comments regarding pastors presuppose that your pastor/bishop/priest meets the qualifications for the office set by God Himself. The discussions herein assume that your pastor is living a sustained holy and righteous life, according to the Holy Bible, and that he is in right standing with God. If he is not, pray that he will either repent and recommit himself to serve the Lord and lead his flock according to the will of God, or that God will lead you to a church that has such a leader.

It is also recognized that in many churches the pastor is a woman rather than a man, or the pastorate is composed of the pastor and his wife, the first lady. However, for simplicity of reading, the pronoun "he" will be used as reference for the office of the pastor).

Chapter One
OLD TESTAMENT LEVITES

¹¹ And Aaron shall offer the Levites before the Lord for an offering of the children of Israel, that they may execute the service of the Lord.

¹⁵ And after that shall the Levites go in to do the service of the tabernacle of the congregation…

¹⁹ And I have given the Levites as a gift to Aaron and to his sons…to do service of the children of Israel in the tabernacle of the congregation… [Numbers 8:11, 15, 19]

I think many people have the wrong idea about church membership. You do not become a member just to fulfill a civic or moral obligation. You do not become a member just to meet and socialize with others. You do not become a member to be entertained by the choir or the pastor and see them perform for your pleasure. You do not become a member for the purpose of obtaining a position and a title. Just like your pastor, priest or bishop, you also have a holy Kingdom work to do for the glory of God. You are called to be a spiritual Levite to your pastor. In order to meet the challenges and responsibilities you may face as a 21st century spiritual Levite, you must understand who the Levites were and the charge given to them by God.

The Levites were the children and descendents of Levi, the third son of Jacob, the patriarch and founder of the twelve tribes of Israel. However, the

Levites were far more than mere members of one of the twelve tribes. They were a chosen people within a chosen people. Moses and his brother Aaron were Levites. As we know, Moses was the Deliverer and the Lawgiver of the Hebrews, and Aaron became the first high priest of the Hebrews, through whom succeeding Hebrew high priests descended. The remaining Levites, who were not direct descendents of Aaron, were especially set aside by God to assist the high priest and his descendents in the performance of the sacred duties attendant to that office, including overseeing the sacred services and governing the maintenance of the holy tabernacle. As the Scriptures above record, Aaron offered the Levites up to God as an offering, and God gave the Levites back to Aaron as a gift, all for the purpose of serving in the house of God. The Levites were, in essence, the first "*helps ministry*", established by God Himself.

A HOLY NATION: A WORK IN PROGRESS

After anointing and using Moses to accomplish the release of the Hebrew people from Egyptian slavery, God gave Moses his next major task. He was charged to form those millions of people who constituted the twelve tribes into one nation called *Israel*. Those former slaves were to be God's earthly ambassadors and a nation of holy people elected to proclaim to the world that Jehovah was the only true God. The Israelites were to lead the world, by precept and example, into holiness unto Jehovah.

However, before they could convey holiness to the rest of the world, they had to become holy themselves. They had to throw off 430 years of compulsion to worship and serve the false gods that had surrounded them throughout their years of slavery. They had to remember the God of their fathers, the God of Abraham, Isaac and Jacob. Many had forgotten Him; some never even knew of Him and His special relationship with the Hebrews. They had to learn how to worship the one true God and how to live holy before Him. The same principle holds true today. Even if you have been chosen and ordained by God to accomplish a holy work for His glory, *you* must first be holy. How can you expect those you minister to or preach to to live a life of holiness if *you* are not living holy?

God, therefore, commissioned Moses to have a holy Tabernacle constructed, wherein the presence of the Lord would dwell among His people, and where they would congregate to worship Him. Just as this tabernacle would be mobile and accompany the nation Israel as the people traversed the desert to the Promised Land, so would the presence of God be with them on their journey.

Moreover, God gave Moses the Ten Commandments as the blueprint for a life of holiness before God and man. God then ordained the office of the high priest to serve as the spiritual leader of the people. Our omniscient Heavenly Father knew that this new congregation required spiritual order and instruction, as well as accountability, in order to become that holy nation fit to carry out the work of the Lord. He knew that, if left to themselves to individually determine what was right and holy by their own standards, the people would become a spiritual shipwreck even before they learned the ways of God.

Aaron, the brother of Moses, was chosen by God to be the first high priest to the people. God stipulated that the office of the high priest, as well as that of the priest, could only be filled by the direct descendents of Aaron. But the remaining Levites who were indirect descendents of Aaron were also consecrated to God to assist the high priest.

> *28Because their office [their duty] was to wait [to help] on the sons of Aaron for the service of the house of the Lord, in the courts, and in the chambers, and in the purifying of all holy things, and the work of the service of the house of God.*
>
> *32And that they should keep [attend to the needs of] the charge of the tabernacle of the congregation, and the charge of the holy place, and the charge of the sons of Aaron their brethren, in the service of the house of the Lord.* [I Chronicles 23:28, 32]

Thus, the Levites had three major categories of responsibility:

1. They were to assist and help the high priest in the conduct of worship services in the house of the Lord, including any preparation required by the high priest for such services. This responsibility had many facets to it.
2. They were to assist and help the high priest in the maintenance and care of the house of God in general, and the sanctuary in particular, in whatever areas and ways the high priest deemed necessary.

3. They were to see to the care of the high priest, so that he could carry out the high responsibility of his office without hindrance or distraction.

The duties were not arbitrarily performed by the Levites; rather, their duties were assigned to them, as well as the schedule they were to follow to perform those duties.

During the years the nation of Israel was in the wilderness, journeying from place to place, the holy Tabernacle had to be moved as well. The Levites, alone, were charged to see to the transportation of the Tabernacle and everything associated with the Tabernacle. At the command of God, certain Levites were assigned to set up the tent of the Tabernacle and dismantle and carry it to the next location. Others were given the responsibility to transport other parts of the Tabernacle, such as the curtains and door hangings, boards, bars, pillars, sockets and cords of the Tabernacle. Certain Levites were assigned to carry the sanctuary of the Tabernacle and the wrapped holy vessels of the sanctuary. However, they were not permitted to wrap the holy vessels; this task was left to the high priest (Aaron) and his sons (the direct descendents of the high priest). Once the holy vessels were wrapped, the Levites were allowed to carry them to the next campsite. By God's decree, if any of them touched the unwrapped holy vessels, they would die. These were the instructions laid down by God Himself and given to Moses to relay to the Levites. (See Numbers 4).

When King David removed the Ark of the Covenant from the house of Obed-Edom and had it carried back to Jerusalem, *"the children of the Levites bare the ark of God upon their shoulders with the staves thereon, as Moses commanded according to the word of the Lord."* [I Chronicles 15:15]. This was the way God commanded that the ark was to be moved; it was:

1) to be carried by Levites,
2) by staves, positioned through rings on the Ark, which were then placed upon their shoulders.

Not only was it forbidden for anyone, including the Levites, to touch the Ark itself; but the Ark could only be transported by Levites personally carrying it on their shoulders.

However, prior to the successful transportation of the Ark to Jerusalem, David had caused the Ark to be transported on a new cart. When the ox stumbled while pulling the cart, causing the Ark to be in danger of falling to the ground, a man named Uzza touched the Ark to steady it and keep it from falling. That seemed to be a good gesture, right? Wrong! God's anger was kindled, not only because the Ark was being transported in a way contrary to His command, but more so because someone had touched the Ark. Many believe that Uzza was not even a Levite; however that would not have mattered -- no human hand was to touch the Ark! *"And the anger of the Lord was kindled against Uzza, and He smote him, because he put his hand to the ark: and there he died before God."* [I Chronicles 13:10].

There are lessons the New Testament church congregation can learn from these passages:

- If you wish to work in and for your local church, make sure your work is assigned or approved by your pastor.
- Do the work or service assigned *to you*.
- Do not touch or handle responsibilities that have not been assigned to you. Your pastor may have had a good reason for not giving the assignment to you. You don't know why someone else was given a particular assignment rather than you. You don't know what instructions God has given your pastor.
- To presumptuously attempt to perform the task, just because you know how, may be viewed as spiritual disobedience in the eyes of God.

THE DUTIES OF THE LEVITES

The duties of the Levites are recorded throughout the Old Testament, and are too numerous to be named here; but some of their responsibilities and positions were as follows:

- Set up, dismantled and transported the tent of the Tabernacle, the Ark of the Covenant, the vessels, the instruments, and other items within the Tabernacle;

- Received the animal sacrifices from the people and prepared them for the high priest to offer up to God on the holy altar;
- Porters, doorkeepers and gatekeepers of the Tabernacle/Temple;
- Singers who sang songs of praise and worship to God, both day and night;
- Musicians who played and accompanied the singers;
- Made the ointment and spices used in the sacred services;
- Prepared the showbread;
- Took care of the vessels used in the sanctuary;
- Offered up prayers of praise and thanksgiving and prayers of petition for the needs of the people;
- Oversaw the treasuries of the house of God;
- Scribes;
- Taught the Law to the people;
- Heard, judged and resolved controversies among the people;
- Warriors who protected the king.

The duties of the Levites were numerous and varied, and they changed as the needs of the high priest and the order of service changed over time. But the mandate and holy charge given to them did not change. They were given by God to the high priest, to be a help to the high priest as they followed him in holy service to the Lord.

Chapter Two
FOLLOW THE LEADER

The act of following is like a two-sided coin. There must be a leader – a person you would want to follow – and there must be followers, those who line up behind the leader, who are in agreement with the leader, and who follow the leader – for the right reasons. Both sides make up the coin.

"Heads" – The Leader: Side One of the Coin

There was a game we played when I was a child, called "Follow the Leader". It was a simple game, with easy to understand rules. You simply followed the designated leader wherever he or she went, and did, in like fashion, whatever the leader did. Sometimes we knew exactly where the leader would take us; sometimes we didn't. Even so, we usually had some idea where he or she was headed. There were times when the leader was not sure of the exact path he would be taking until he started going; but he knew the general direction. And we followed.

Now, a good leader (i.e., one we could trust) did not take us anywhere that was too dangerous, or to places we knew our parents forbade us to go to. Let me make this plain: **we did not just follow some nut in our group**. We only followed one who was worthy of our trust. But with that established, yes, we did take on some challenges while following the leader. That was part of the adventure.

In this game you had to stay close to the group and keep your eyes on the leader; otherwise, you might end up left behind, lost and unable to find the leader or your group. If that happened, well . . . the game was over for you. The wonderful thing about this game was that any number of people who wanted to play by the rules of the game could play.

Now, I don't know about your group of childhood playmates, but when my group of friends played this game of "Follow the Leader", **we never got into trouble with our parents for doing so, and we always arrived safely at our destination at the end of the game.**

I was thinking about this game and how, in many ways, it resembles following the shepherd God designated to be the head of your church and the watcher for your soul. However, unlike the childhood game, your soul salvation and your commitment to God Almighty is not a game. You cannot afford to follow just anyone in this Christian walk – not if you plan to hear the words, *"Well done, My good and faithful servant"* on Judgment Day, and spend eternity with God.

You need to earnestly seek the counsel and guidance of God concerning the leader you are to follow. It doesn't matter whether they go by the title of Apostle, Bishop, Prophet or Prophetess, Evangelist, Priest, Pastor or Teacher; they had better line up with the holy word of God in both their preaching (feeding the sheep) and in the conduct of their lives (holiness) if you are going to trust them to watch over your soul.

My pastor and first lady *do* line up with the Word and have lived holy lives before God and man ever since each of them was saved years ago. As of this writing, my pastor has been saved and consistently living a saved life for over 40 years. My first lady has been saved and consistently living a saved life for over 47 years. Together they have been pastoring a church (now in two states) for over 27 years. They have been proven to be obedient and holy servants of God, *chosen by God* to shepherd and lead God's people, and, more personally, to shepherd and lead me.

I have been a member of their church and under their leadership for 25 years and I know without a shadow of a doubt that God planted me under their leadership. I know, without wavering, that God placed my on-going salvation into their spiritual care. I have no problem entrusting my soul to their watch care. So, yes, I can "follow the leader". You see, I follow them as they follow Christ. They are holy; they are righteous; they are humble; they are loving; they are trustworthy; they are highly anointed. Are they perfect? No, but they are faithful, committed, submitted, obedient, morally and spiritually clean servants of God . . . and they are rare. I count it a privilege to follow them and serve as a spiritual Levite to them. I consider it my responsibility to undergird them, protect them, and be a help to them in whatever way they or God directs me, as they lead us to carry out God's Kingdom work in these end times.

If you can say the same about your pastor and first lady, please examine yourself as you continue to read this book, to make sure you are doing *your* Levitical *part* in the Kingdom work given your pastor and your church. If you cannot say the same things about your pastor and first lady, please close this book *immediately* and pray to God for guidance.

"Tails" - The Follower: Side Two of the Coin

Now, for those of you who can continue to read this section, let me make this clarification about following your leader: Following someone and walking behind someone are not the same. You can walk behind someone, even among many others who are following that same person, and yet not be a follower yourself. Just because you are a member of a church congregation does not mean that you are necessarily a follower of the shepherd of that congregation. You see, I define and regard a follower as someone who has the same spiritual heart as the leader and one who is of the same spiritual mindset as the leader. Sometimes they are in close physical proximity to the leader, sometimes not. But the deciding factor is the state of their heart. The relevant and initial act of "followship" takes place in the heart. If their heart is not with the leader, if the best interest of their Christ-led leader is not a prevailing dynamic in their spiritual (and natural) heart, they are not a follower. And if you are not a follower, I have to ask the question: *Why are you there? What is your purpose? Do you have a hidden agenda?* I'm just asking.

Consider Gehazi, the personal servant, traveling companion and confidante of that great prophet Elisha. We know that before Elisha left everything to follow the prophet Elijah; he had servants whom he knew well; servants who regularly worked with him in his father's fields. We also read that after Elijah's death, and just prior to the onset of his own prophetic ministry, Elisha had encounters with the "sons of the prophets". Yet it was Gehazi, alone, who had the privilege of accompanying this chosen man of God throughout his travels, ministering to him and even assisting him in the work God had set before Elisha. Holy Scripture does not reveal whether Gehazi was even one of the sons of the prophets, and yet he was able to witness the performance of miracles by Elisha that others were not able to see. He had the opportunity to glean spiritual revelation, insight and wisdom at the feet of Elisha as he traveled everywhere with the prophet. He had the opportunity to serve a great man of God, a chosen vessel, by endeavoring to make the prophet's great responsibilities easier to bear. At first glance, it looks as if Gehazi "followed" Elisha. Perhaps, initially he did.

And yet, at some point there was a turning in Gehazi and he was no longer in harmony with Elisha's heart, spirit or best interests. Gehazi had his own hidden agenda and motives for "following" Elisha. Gehazi sought to promote himself and obtain riches for himself by taking unrighteous advantage of his position as the close companion and confidante of Elisha, even to the point of lying *on* and lying *to* the prophet.

Chapter Five of the Book of Second Kings records that after Elisha healed Naaman, the captain of the Syrian army, the prophet refused to accept gifts offered by Naaman as thanksgiving for his healing. Gehazi was standing right there with the prophet and heard Elisha say, *"As the Lord liveth, before whom I stand, I will receive none."* [2 Kings 5:16]. The Scripture continues:

> [20] *But Gehazi, the servant of Elisha the man of God, said, Behold, my master hath spared Naaman this Syrian, in not receiving at his hands that which he brought: but as the Lord liveth, I will run after him, and take somewhat of him.*
>
> [21] *So Gehazi followed after Naaman. And when Naaman saw him running after him, he lighted down from the chariot, to meet him, and said, Is all well?*

²² And he said, All is well. My master hath sent me, saying, Behold, even now there be come to me from mount Ephraim two young men of the sons of the prophets; give them, I pray thee, a talent of silver, and two changes of garments. [2 Kings 5:20-22]

Lies, lies, lies! Elisha never sent Gehazi back to Naaman. There were no sons of the prophet coming to see Elisha. Elisha did not tell Gehazi to ask Naaman for money and clothing for these two imaginary visitors. Gehazi just lied **on** the prophet. But unsaved Naaman had more integrity and honesty than Gehazi; he gave Gehazi not just one talent but two talents of silver, in addition to the requested garments.

Gehazi brought the money and clothing back to Elisha's camp . . . but not to Elisha. Nor did he tell Elisha what he had just done. *"But he went in, and stood before his master. And Elisha said unto him, Whence comest thou, Gehazi? And he said, Thy servant went no whither."* [2 Kings 5:25]. More lies by Gehazi; except this time he lied **to** the prophet.

He not only lied on the prophet and to the prophet, he could not even say he did it for the benefit of the prophet (which still would have been unrighteous). Gehazi appropriated the money and clothes for himself (I call it theft by a scam artist); and what's worse, he used his position with the man of God to do so. Despite his close physical proximity and duties to the prophet, Gehazi's actions did not reflect those of a true follower. Neither his heart, interests, spirit nor vision lined up with Elisha.

The same can be said of the Hebrews who were delivered out of slavery. Millions of newly freed Hebrews walked behind Moses, as he led them away from Egypt and slavery and toward the Promised Land. But only two of the adults actually "followed" him. The rest never kept Moses' spirit or his best interests in their hearts. They never had confidence that Moses was God's chosen leader for them, even though God (not Moses) had proven this to them time and time again. They never consistently cooperated with Moses as he carried out this most difficult task.

Their constant grumbling, complaining and opposition to Moses, even as he continued to lead them further and further away from slavery and closer and closer to the full promise of God, testified against them as evidence of their failure to "follow". These grumblers were in the midst of the congregation; they were in the presence of their leader; but they were never "with" their leader. They walked behind, but they never followed.

Following the God-chosen spiritual leader for your life requires that both sides of the coin – the shepherd and the congregation member – line up with the will of God, the One who created the coin. Are you following your pastor or are you just walking behind him? Are you both following Christ? I'm just asking.

Chapter Three

GOD ORDAINED THE OFFICE OF THE PASTOR

In order to be a good Christian follower you have to have a good Christian pastor, one chosen by God. I honor God, Who is truly the Head of my life. I honor my Lord and Savior Jesus Christ. I honor the precious Holy Ghost. I also give honor to the leaders God chose and shaped to be the shepherds and watchers over my soul – my pastor and his wife, my first lady.

I honor the Triune Godhead, because if it had not been for God the Father, God the Son and God the Holy Ghost, I would not have been saved, sanctified and filled with the Holy Ghost. And yes, I honor my pastor and first lady, because if it had not been for them (who jointly form the pastorate of my church) I would not be yet saved, yet sanctified, yet filled with the Holy Ghost, living a sustained life of holiness and walking in the knowledge of how to serve God in a way that pleases Him.

God the Father, the Creator of all, created me out of His love. When sin came into the world and separated us from relationship with God the Father, this loving Father sent God the Son, Jesus Christ, to be a sacrificial lamb for our sake. Jesus was the only acceptable sacrifice to reconcile mankind to God the Father. Jesus lovingly and willingly humbled Himself to be born into this world to reveal the character and commands of the Holy Father. Through His righteous life and holy gospel, Jesus showed us how to live righteously all the days of our lives. His great desire has always been that we attain to the place of sonship with the Father and spend eternity with Him.

The love did not stop there.

Upon His ascension to glory after His resurrection from death, Jesus committed to intercede for us continuously, as our great High Priest, from His seat right next to God the Father. As He took His holy seat, our Lord sent the Holy Ghost to dwell within us as our ever-present Comforter and Guide, to help us maintain a consistent walk of holiness while yet in this world.

Oh yes, if God had not saved me I would not have been saved and spiritually reborn. But you know that water baptism and rebirth in Christ is only the very beginning of a life as a Christian – I mean as a true Christian; one who strives to spiritually live as Jesus Christ did; one who lives to obey the commandments of God; one who seeks to please God and glorify His name throughout their life.

Our wise and all-knowing God knew that as willing as our spirits were, our flesh would be weak…and the devil would be busy. God knew that even with true repentance for our sins, salvation of our souls, rebirth in Christ Jesus, and the indwelling Holy Ghost, we earthen vessels would yet need additional help to keep us on the right path. And so, He gave us another safeguard; He gave us pastors. For He said: *"And I will give you pastors [shepherds] according to Mine heart, which shall feed you with knowledge and understanding."* [Jeremiah 3:15]. The word of God also says:

> *⁸ Wherefore He saith, WHEN HE ASCENDED UP ON HIGH, HE LED CAPTIVITY CAPTIVE AND GAVE GIFTS UNTO MEN.*
>
> *¹¹ And He gave some, apostles; and some, prophets; and some, evangelists; and some, pastors and teachers;*
>
> *¹² For the perfecting of the saints, for the work of the ministry, for the edifying of the body of Christ* [Ephesians 4:8, 11-12]

God gave the Church pastors, and He did it for a three-fold purpose:

- To perfect the saints [i.e., guide them to spiritual maturity];
- **For the work of the ministry;**
- For the edifying [building up] of the body of Christ.

That is the command to the pastors.

Because God gave such "gifts" to the Church, He instructs the congregation, through the Book of Hebrews 13:17, *"Obey them that have the rule over you, and submit yourselves: for they watch for your souls, as they must give account, that they may do it with joy, and not grief: for that is unprofitable for you."*

That is God's command to the congregation. Not only are you to obey and submit to the rule of your pastor (one who reflects God's heart), but you have an obligation to be a joy for the pastor to lead and not someone who constantly grieves the pastor.

Thus, you see it is a biblical truth that you need a pastor to govern your spiritual life in Christ. It is not unlike the need for a baby to have parents to watch over that child's natural life, govern the progress of that child's life, and strive to ensure that it reaches adulthood safely, fully equipped to face the world. A good parent will provide or try to provide the child with everything he needs, but not necessarily everything he wants. Sometimes the things children want are harmful rather than helpful.

Note, however, that the Scriptures make clear that God is the One to give you your pastor. Man is not to designate himself as a "self-proclaimed" pastor. Nor should your pastor be the shepherd and hold that holy office because of his popularity, his financial standing, his influence, his social or political prestige, his looks, his contacts or any other carnal reasons.

Being a pastor is not a job or a career choice. It is not something one chooses in order to avoid secular employment. It is not an option he can choose in order to satisfy his ego by being the "boss" over everyone else or the controller of a congregation in order to further his own personal agenda. And the office most certainly was not ordained by God as a way for a man to meet and/or interact with a number of women. (Oh, grow up, please – we know that some false pastors entered the pastorate for this very reason.) One cannot even decide to become a pastor just because he loves God and the people of God.

Lawful entry into the office of the pastorate requires that one must be called, chosen and ordained *by God* for this. It is a *calling*, a *Divine* appointment. The pastor is an "undershepherd" of Jesus Christ, the Chief Shepherd. The pastor recognizes that, as the undershepherd to the flock, he represents the Chief Shepherd and is accountable to the Chief Shepherd.

The way the congregation (you) treats the undershepherd (your pastor **who follows Christ**) is an indication of how the congregation (again, you) regards the appointment made by the Chief Shepherd (Christ Jesus), and how the congregation (uh-huh, you) regards Jesus Himself. Think about this from now on as you interact with your pastor, do things for your pastor (or refrain from doing things for him), obey or disobey your pastor, and communicate with others about your pastor. (Again, however, I remind you of the caveat you read earlier: If your pastor is not living a holy life before God and man, as the word of God requires, and in fact has chosen to lead a life in disobedience or rebellion to God's commands, please, please do not follow him down that path. That road will lead you to hell…along with the one you are following.)

Chapter Four
WHAT'S WRONG WITH HAVING A PASTOR?

Alright... now, knowing that even as children we played the game of "Follow the Leader" and saw no problem with that, and knowing that God ordained the office of the pastor, let me place this next question under the spiritual microscope for examination: Why do we have a problem when it comes to acknowledging, respecting, obeying and following a church shepherd, i.e., the pastorate? Why do the hairs on the back of our necks bristle and our tempers flare when it comes to following the instructions of a holy and righteous pastor? Why do some consider it belittling and a personal insult to have to follow the rules and instructions established by the pastor of their local church? I mean, we will readily follow the instructions of others in our lives without ever questioning them.

If your doctor writes a prescription for you and tells you to take some medicine, you run to the pharmacy to get the prescription filled. You take the medicine faithfully even though it comes with warnings that the side effects may be worse than your affliction. You take the medicine even though you don't really understand what it is composed of. You take the medicine even though you have no idea what you are ingesting into your body. You can't even pronounce or spell the name of the medicine.

You don't put the doctor through the third degree about his medical background and expertise (no you don't). Reading his certificate and the license hanging prominently on the wall does not tell you if he is really qualified to treat you, or how qualified he is. It doesn't tell you if he even knows what he is talking about. But you don't tell him how he should treat your medical condition. You just obey the doctor and take the medicine. Why? Because you want to be well and you trust your doctor.

When you are hired for a job and given your job description, or when your supervisor at your job gives you instructions, you don't ask him what right he has to give you orders, do you? (If you do, I can assume you are or will be among the ranks of the unemployed who were fired from their jobs for insubordination). You may not understand why your supervisor wants you to do what you are instructed to do. You may not be given all the whys and wherefores underlying the task assigned. Your boss may not have asked for your input concerning the instructions given to you. But if the task is legal, within the reasonable expectations of your particular position or duties, is not harmful or against your moral conscience and is one you are capable of doing, most of you will obey your supervisor and do what is assigned to you. You may not like what you are doing. You may not even like your boss, but you do the job. Why? Because you want that paycheck and the benefits that come with it.

Think about this: We will even obey inanimate objects, things that are not even human. When most of us are driving and come to a red light, we stop. With or without the nearby presence of a police officer, we stop. There is no one there telling us to stop; there may not even be anyone there to witness whether we stop or not. But we obey some colored lights that are embedded in a steel pole or overhanging fixture. The lights do not even know you are there. Yet we accept the authority of this inanimate object to tell us how and when we can drive the car that we paid for! Why? Because we don't want to get hit or harmed by someone coming from another direction. Or, because we don't want to get pulled over by an officer who was observing us from a hidden vantage point, with his ticket citation book on the seat of his patrol car.

But when it comes to obeying a Spirit-filled, God-ordained righteous and holy person, chosen by God to be your pastor and spiritual leader, we have all kinds of attitude problems. We don't think they should have any authority over us, when the Bible we *say* we study and agree with clearly says, *"Obey them that have the rule over you, and submit yourselves..."*

[Hebrews 13:17]. God commands us to do this; moreover, He is so gracious that He tells us why we should obey them and submit to them:

> *"...for they watch for your souls, as they must give account, that they may do it with joy, and not grief: for that is unprofitable for you."* [Hebrews 13:17]

Do you see what you just read? Your pastor is not there to just indiscriminately order people around so he can feel important. He is not there to walk around the church with his chest poked out, as his flock says "God bless you, Pastor" when he walks by. He is not there to satisfy his pride, or to exploit, abuse or "control" others. *He is under Divine orders from God to watch for your soul.* Neither your doctor, your employer, nor those traffic lights have this responsibility; nor do they care what happens to your soul.

That means your pastor has to fight *your* demons – you know, the ones that come to attack *you* to hinder *you* from living a holy life, or from receiving the blessings God has for *you*, or from fulfilling the destiny God ordained for *your* life.

That means your pastor has to constantly watch over *you* and his entire congregation, and do his best to keep *each one of you* on the straight and narrow Way of this Christian journey, so that *you* can make it to Heaven and spend eternity with God.

That means your pastor has to sacrifice precious hours of sleep, to pray or war throughout the night, on *your* behalf, while you rest and snore, oblivious to his intercession and the fact that demons are after *you*. Or your pastor fasts often, resisting the temptation to eat, even though he is hungry, in order to get a timely word from God for *you* and the rest of the congregation. And he often has done this without you ever having known that he did.

God not only commands your pastor to do all that is necessary to watch for your soul, but He admonishes him that on Judgment Day he must give an account to God. He must account not only for what **he** did or did not do to watch for your soul, but how well **you** responded and submitted to his rule over you as he watched for your very precious soul. Oh-oh!

Was it a joy for the pastor to watch over you, because of your willing submission and good attitude, or was it grievous because of your rebellion and contentious attitude? That is the question God will ask your pastor concerning you. And believe me, a righteous pastor carries great weight and favor with God, far more than you and I, so his answers will matter. Don't think you and your pastor are on the same level of relationship with God. God and His shepherds have a special relationship the congregation must recognize, accept and honor.

YOU ARE NOT ON THE SAME LEVEL AS YOUR PASTOR.

Oh, let us stay right here for a moment. If you think you have the same relationship with God that your pastor has, you need to re-read the Books of Exodus, Numbers and Deuteronomy. Begin with a study of how God dealt with Miriam and Aaron when those two entertained and acted upon the false presumption that they were equal to Moses in their relationship with God.

As a child, Miriam was used by God to save the infant Moses from death, in order that he might be preserved for his great destiny. Her act of saving that baby enabled that baby to reach adulthood and free millions of God's chosen people from 430 years of continuous slavery to a heathen nation. As an adult, during her peoples' "freedom walk", Miriam was a prophetess and the praise leader of millions of Hebrews. Her brother, Aaron, was by Moses' side when Moses confronted Pharaoh ten times and demanded the release of all of the Hebrew slaves. Moreover, Aaron was the first high priest of the newly formed nation of Israel, chosen by Jehovah to hold that office and oversee the spiritual activities of the people during their wilderness journey. *But Miriam and Aaron were not Moses.*

Yes, Moses was their brother and their baby brother at that; but first and foremost he was God's chosen leader of this special, called-out people. He was appointed to lead millions of newly freed people – including Miriam and Aaron – out of Egypt and slavery and into the Promised Land and the will of God.

Moses was the one God ordained to form a nation out of former slaves who knew nothing about freedom and independence, and to transform them into the holy people God elected them to be.

Moses was the one given the charge and spiritual authority to confront Pharaoh and demand that he let the people go.

Moses was the one given power from God to bring about ten plagues that fell upon Egypt but not upon Goshen.

Moses was the one God spoke to and gave the strategy to for the release of His people.

If the ten plagues were not enough, the miraculous parting of the Red Sea at the command of **Moses** should have been more than sufficient to firmly convince the people of Moses' special relationship with God.

Time and time again, when the people were in need in the wilderness for forty years, it was **Moses** through whom God acted to supply their need.

Moses' prayers to God caused the multitude to be fed with food (manna, and meat, no less) and water, when none was to be found in the desert.

Moses was the one God called up to Mt. Sinai to receive the Ten Commandments to give to the people.

Moses was the one permitted to commune alone with God for forty days and forty nights – twice.

It was the uplifted arms of **Moses** that led to victory for the Israelites when they engaged in a battle with the Amalekites in the wilderness.

Moses was the one to whom God spoke face-to-face.

As you study these books of the Bible you see that, again and again, God affirmed and confirmed to the millions of Israelites that Moses was God's choice to lead and shepherd this nation of Israel whom God loved.

Do you remember the words of Miriam and Aaron when they contended against Moses' leadership? Do you remember God's reply when He rebuked them for opposing Moses, and the punishment He imposed on Miriam, the ringleader?

> *²And they said, Hath the Lord indeed spoken only by Moses? hath He not spoken by us? And the Lord heard it.*

> *⁶ And He said, Hear now My words: If there be a prophet among you, I the Lord will make Myself known unto him in a vision, and will speak unto him in a dream.*
>
> *⁷ My servant Moses is not so, who is faithful in all Mine house,*
>
> *⁸ With him will I speak mouth to mouth, even apparently and not in dark speeches; and the similitude of the Lord shall he behold: wherefore were ye not afraid to speak against My servant Moses?* [Numbers 12:2, 6-8]

Note carefully the words in verse two. It says that God heard their conversation. Miriam and Aaron were talking to each other, not to God; but God heard them. Moses did not hear them; he wasn't even aware that his siblings felt as they did; but God heard. *God heard. GOD HEARD!* It always amazes me that people think they can hide their words, actions, and even their thoughts from an Omniscient God. Note also that even though the words Miriam and Aaron spoke were not critical of God, God was angry because the words were an offense to Moses, God's prophet. Just think about that the next time you want to badmouth a righteous pastor for obeying God rather than you.

As you will recall, Miriam was then stricken with leprosy and had to be put outside of the camp, separated from the rest of the nation. I'm sure she cried out to God for healing, but her cries were ineffective to remove the leprosy. It was only because of **Moses'** intercession on her behalf that she was healed of this dreadful, incurable disease. If Moses, the leader, the pastor, had not petitioned God on her behalf, Miriam may have remained a leper, consigned to remain outside of the camp and the presence of God, for the rest of her life. (See Numbers 12:1-15)

Thank God for a compassionate shepherd who loved his flock and had a special relationship with God.

Let us also consider Korah and his little posse. Like Miriam and Aaron, this group had also witnessed the many signs, wonders and miracles God had performed through Moses to deliver the Hebrews out of slavery. Korah's little gang also opposed Moses, but they went a step further than Miriam and Aaron. They not only challenged Moses' leadership among themselves, they tried to turn the rest of the congregation against Moses. And many of the people actually listened to them and agreed with them. But in their unabashed opposition to Moses, Korah and his conspirators were really fighting against God… and God dealt with them. (See Numbers 16:1-33).

Now, these fickle followers of Korah never considered the fact that during all the years they had been slaves in Egypt Korah never presented a plan or professed to have been given a strategy or charge from God to deliver the people out of slavery. The people never had any evidence that God was working signs, wonders and miracles through Korah. That is because God never did work any signs, wonders or miracles through Korah. The people never had any indication that Korah prayed to God or sought His counsel. In fact, there was never an inkling that God even spoke to Korah…ever!

God did not use Korah to confront Pharaoh; or to free the Hebrews from slavery; or to part the Red Sea; or to provide the multitude with food from out of nowhere in the wilderness; or to produce water out of a rock, where before there was no water in sight. Korah did not even deliver himself from Egypt and slavery.

Yet these double-minded folks began to prefer Korah over Moses. The multitude really had no evidence to support this sudden confidence in Korah but, rather, had every reason to dismiss his complaints and challenges to Moses' God-given authority. Still, they rallied around Korah instead of God's proven leader who had been used to free them. Does that make any sense at all?

So, here we had Miriam, Aaron and Korah, self-proclaimed "leader wannabees" who had no strategy or help from God for the preservation of a freed people, but who complained about and opposed the one who did. They saw Moses' leadership as a problem, but they had no real solution.

Wasn't it enough for Miriam, Aaron, Korah and the rest of the naysayers to know that they were part of a chosen people? Wasn't it enough for them to know that God loved them so much that He sent one to rescue them out of 430 years of bondage? Did they ever stop to consider and appreciate that Moses made a huge sacrifice to obey God and serve as the leader of the nation of Israel, all for their benefit? I'm just asking.

After all, Moses had already escaped the chains of Egyptian slavery. For forty years he had been living a peaceful, contented, family-oriented life. He was already free! From a non-spiritual point of view, he had absolutely nothing to gain by retracing his steps and making an arduous, round trip journey across the dry, hot, merciless desert to Egypt, to obtain freedom for some other folks. (*Sidebar*: Moses might have said *"No way"* instead of obeying God, if he had had prior knowledge of the headaches awaiting him as the Deliverer of these complaining, murmuring folk. Maybe that's why God has to show us the roadmap of our destiny little by little, without giving us all the details.)

But God did not command Moses to give up his peaceful life and go back to Egypt for Moses' sake. He sent him back for the sake of the millions of Hebrews who were still in bondage. He sent him back for the sake of His beloved people, whose tearful supplications for deliverance had been heard and felt by God. Thank God Moses said *"yes"* to God's command.

A true pastor gives up much for the sake of the flock God has entrusted to his care.

Didn't Moses, then, deserve the prayers and cooperation of those he led and loved? Didn't he deserve whatever help the people could have given him to make his monumental task a little easier to bear and complete? Didn't he deserve their respect for the authority God had given him and his humble use of that authority? Didn't he deserve their respect for the anointing and power of God that was so very evident upon him? Didn't he deserve their respect as the one God chose to be the leader/pastor of the people?

Didn't God deserve that respect?

I think so. Joshua and Caleb thought so too.

JOSHUA AND CALEB

Joshua held a very prestigious and important position with Moses, just as did Miriam and Aaron. Joshua was Moses' minister (servant) and armor bearer in the wilderness. Through his relationship with Moses, Joshua was privileged to see and experience things of God which the rest of the Israelites never saw or experienced; Aaron also enjoyed that privilege. Joshua was privy to Moses' private, personal relationship with Jehovah; so were Miriam and Aaron.

And yet, Joshua never tried to usurp Moses' position with God or with the people, as did Aaron and Korah. Joshua never presumed to think that because he was Moses' personal minister and armor bearer he had the same type of relationship with God Moses had; on the other hand, Miriam was guilty of making this presumption about herself.

When God called Moses to Mount Sinai to receive the Ten Commandments, only Joshua was allowed to accompany him. And yet, when Moses told Joshua he could go no further than the foot of the mountain, Joshua obeyed. He did not get an attitude or feel rebuffed. Instead, he remained at the foot of the mountain while Moses continued his ascent to meet God. (See Exodus 24:1-2, 12-13 and 32:15-17). Joshua waited there day and night, enduring the hot desert sun and cold desert nights, until Moses returned. Joshua probably had to ration his water and food, because neither he nor Moses knew how long this summons from God would last; and indeed, it lasted for 40 days and 40 nights. But Joshua patiently waited for the return of the man of God.

Joshua knew he had a special place with Moses. I'm sure Joshua knew that the multitude of Israelites were aware of this as well. Yet:

- Joshua never tried to displace Moses as the leader;
- He never tried to persuade the people to follow him instead of Moses;
- He never tried to turn the people against Moses;
- He never challenged Moses' authority or instructions;
- He never ignored or countermanded Moses' instructions;
- He never tried to sabotage Moses' work;
- He never even complained to Moses or irritated him.

On the contrary, he endeavored to support Moses in whatever way he could, so that Moses could obey God and carry out every command God gave to him. Why? Because Joshua not only *recognized* that Moses, alone, had been chosen by God to lead and pastor the people, but Joshua *accepted* the will of God.

Joshua also had sense enough to understand that because Moses was obeying God, all of the Hebrews had been delivered from slavery and were being preserved in that merciless desert. Joshua understood that God was leading Moses and Moses was following God. Hence, Joshua rightly discerned and concluded that it would be in his best interest to line up with Moses and follow, undergird and protect this man of God as much as he could.

Joshua had no problem being a follower of a great, chosen, holy, righteous and obedient servant of God Almighty.

The same can be said about Caleb. I just love Caleb. Moses had selected him along with Joshua and ten others, and told them to go spy out the Promised Land and bring back a report on the conditions of the land and the people. He also told them to bring back some of the fruit from the land. Caleb did not hesitate to say "yes" to the command nor did he ask for any additional details. (See Numbers 13 and 14). You see, Caleb trusted his leader. This was not blind trust; on the contrary, he had every reason to trust Moses. Moses didn't have to prove himself to Caleb. He didn't have to convince Caleb that he had heard from God and could lead the people according to the will of God. God had already proven that to Caleb; therefore, Caleb saw no reason to delay.

The twelve spies were gone for forty days into enemy territory, and *all came back alive, unhurt and undetected* by the Canaanites. Not only that, they brought back pomegranates and figs, and grapes that were so huge it took two men to carry one branch of the grapes! And yet, even while they stood before Moses and the congregation, holding in their hands the evidence that God was with them, ten of them wallowed in fear and self-defeat, protesting that the Canaanites were too much for them to conquer. But what did Caleb and Joshua say to them?

> [8] *If the Lord delight in us, then He will bring us into this land, and give it us; a land which floweth with milk and honey.*

⁹ Only rebel not ye against the Lord . . [Numbers 14:8-9]

"Only rebel not ye against the Lord." That is interesting. Caleb did not warn the people to refrain from rebelling against Moses; he warned them not rebel against the Lord. You see, he knew Moses would only have sent them to spy out the land if God had told him to do so. Caleb knew that by rebelling against Moses, the people were really rebelling against the Lord. Wise Caleb was not going to box with God or His chosen vessel.

Moreover, Caleb was not going to be intimidated by peer pressure. He didn't care what the ten spies and the rest of the congregation said. On the contrary, Caleb may have thought to himself, *"Thank God for preservation in the desert, but I would like to dwell in the land of milk and honey. God's servant said now we can go conquer the inhabitants and possess the land, so let's go, let's get started."* (Modern translation: *"Thank you Lord for this Spam®, but if I can eat filet mignon, and the host said I can have filet mignon…I'll take the filet mignon!"*). In fact, the Bible says his exact words were, *"Let us go up at once and possess it; for we are well able to overcome it."* [Numbers 13:30].

Caleb was ready to conquer and possess the land even before they had spied it out. That's how great his confidence and trust was in God and his leader, Moses. Caleb was going to follow the commands of his shepherd (pastor), the one God chose to speak for Him, regardless of the naysayers.

Joshua and Caleb were the only adults of that first generation who continuously followed, supported, defended and served the man of God and did not grieve his spirit. They were the only adults of that generation who made it into the Promised Land to receive and enjoy the promises of God. By God's decree, Joshua became Moses' successor as leader of the people after Moses died. Joshua was blessed with God's promise that He would be with Joshua as He had been with Moses. Caleb conquered and took the mountain that had been promised him by Moses, God's spokesman. All of this occurred because they followed, obeyed, defended and served God's chosen leader, their pastor and shepherd as it were, in ways that pleased God. They saw the wisdom of submitting to a Divinely-chosen leader who would shepherd them into their destiny and God's will for their lives. They followed the leader as their leader followed God.

Chapter Five
GOD IS A GOD OF ORDER

No one can deny that Moses faced innumerable problems and challenges as he led the newly freed Hebrews toward the Promised Land. Besides facing the merciless desert, Moses had to suffer a fickle, double-minded people. Their entire conversations seemed to be one long, repetitive, nerve-wracking complaint. From:

> "Moses, we are hungry and we have nothing to eat. We are thirsty and there is no water anywhere. Where are you taking us? Why did we listen to you? You brought us here to die."

to:

> "Moses, you prayed to Yahweh and now He has given us manna to eat, which nourishes us every day. We have as much as we need for each day. We have meat to eat, more than we can consume, and we did not even have to hunt for it. You gave us water . . . in the desert... out of a rock. Alright Moses, you know what you are doing. God speaks to you. Tell us what to do and we will obey. You da man, Moses!"

to:

> *"Moses, we are tired of eating this same old manna, day in*
> *and day out, year in and year out, even if it does sustain us*
> *and keep us healthy. Why did we ever leave that wonderful*
> *life of slavery in Egypt and follow you in the first place?"* Wa-
> wa-wa! *Boo-hoo, boo-hoo!*

Day in and day out for forty years (approximately 14,600 days and nights) Moses had to hear this. Just hearing the complaints of an ungrateful people was burden enough for him. Even so, in spite of the complaints and unbelief of the newly-freed adult Israelites, their children -- the second generation of freed slaves -- made it to the doorway of the Promised Land and ultimately entered in, because Moses followed God and led them. By the way, that first generation of freed people – the complaining "goats" – was barred from entering God's Promised Land. Except for Joshua and Caleb, all died because of their murmuring, complaining and unbelief.

OK, now go look in the mirror and examine yourself. Do you see a goat or a lamb looking back at you? I'm just asking. This is a good time for a pregnant pause, a SELAH moment. You may not be barred from physically entering a geographical location, but you may be barred from entering into your destiny. You may not die naturally, but you may die spiritually because of the way you serve or don't serve, follow or don't follow, obey or don't obey spiritual shepherds who are following Christ.

Can you imagine what the consequences would have been if God had delivered these millions of Hebrews from Egyptian slavery, only to release them to the desert wilderness without a leader? Keep in mind that only Moses knew where they were supposed to go; only Moses knew the challenges of the desert that awaited them. It really hurts the brain and heart to even imagine what the outcome would have been had we read that God released the multitude into the desert, without a leader or a plan, and said, *"Go for it; you're on your own, but I still expect you to become a holy nation."* We would have assuredly concluded that the Exodus had never been the will of God. There would have been utter chaos; there would have been confusion. And if there is confusion in your church, believe me – no believe the word of God -- it is not the will of God. *"For God is not the author of confusion, but of peace, as in all churches of the saints."* [1 Corinthians 14:33]

Our God has so many attributes and characteristics, but confusion is not one of them. The first and foremost trait God ever revealed about Himself is that He is a Creator. Even the youngest Christian convert can see and receive this revelation merely by reading the first two chapters of Genesis, the first book of the Bible. What many saints overlook or fail to appreciate and accept is the second thing God revealed about Himself -- He is a God of order, not confusion, fate, luck or happenstance. Even in His creative mode God was a God of order. He created the universe, the earth, and everything in this earth, including mankind, in an orderly fashion.

God took six days to bring into existence what He, alone, created. He could have done it all in one day if He had so chosen, because, after all, He is God and nothing is impossible for Him. But He didn't. Mankind is His most treasured creation and the last thing He created. By the time He brought mankind into existence He had already created everything mankind would need. The light, sun, moon, stars, water, air, trees, flowers, shrubs, herbs, fruit, birds, fish, animals, mountains, valleys, rivers, seas, beautiful landscapes, and more, were all in place for man's pleasure and delight. Man did not want for anything because God had created man's earthly homeland in an orderly manner. It was indeed Paradise.

But God's exercise of order did not stop with the physical creation of this earth. He also ordained that order was to prevail in the affairs of men, especially amongst the Israelites, the people God first sanctified (set apart) to do a special work for Him. Let us look again at Moses and examine God's order, as Moses and the millions of Hebrews journeyed to the Promised Land.

The Beauty of Order

God anointed and appointed Moses to do much more than obtain freedom for the Hebrew people and then lead the way across the desert to a new place to live. Moses was also to lead them into their destiny and the fulfillment of a prophetic promise God made to their patriarchs, Abraham,

Isaac and Jacob. Upon emancipation, the freed people were **twelve** separate tribal descendents of the twelve sons of Jacob; but they were to become **one** nation.

They had been born into slavery and they knew nothing but slavery. They had been subject to the laws and dictates of a country that worshiped many "gods". Many of the Hebrews never knew, had forgotten or no longer reverenced their own God, Yahweh, the only true God, the God of Abraham, Isaac and Jacob. They had no voice concerning the affairs of their own lives. They didn't know how to govern themselves *as a people*. But now, as they made their way toward their destiny, they were to become their own nation. Moreover, they were to become a *holy* nation, one that would worship, serve and bring glory to Yahweh. As a holy nation, they were to reveal the sovereignty of Almighty God to the rest of the world. God had an orderly plan for this people to become that holy nation.

One of the first things God required them to do in the wilderness was to construct and erect a holy Tabernacle, where all the people could assemble as one, to offer sacrifices, prayers, praise and worship to God, and receive instruction from God's spokesman concerning their lives. This building project was a huge endeavor. (See Exodus 25 – 27). The command and the plans for its construction were given to Moses, but it was too big for one man, one family or even one tribe to accomplish alone. Duties had to be divided and delegated. Everything for the Tabernacle had to be made, including:

- The tent of the Tabernacle (which had to have been enormous)
- Boards for the sides of the tent
- Sockets under the boards
- Doors
- Pillars
- The Ark of the Covenant
- Staves for the Ark
- Rings for the staves
- Curtains
- Loops for the curtains
- The veil
- Brass laver

- Gold cherubim
- Coverings for the tent
- Furniture of various shapes and sizes
- Lamps
- Altars
- Vessels
- Dishes
- Spoons
- Candlesticks
- Pots
- Shovels
- Basins
- Flesh hooks
- Fire pans
- Pins
- Holy anointing oil
- Priests' garments

There was no Home Depot®, Lowe's® or Sears® to go to for the purchase of these items. They had to be made and they all had to be made accurately, according to God's succinct commands.

God had given the vision and exact instructions for the construction of the Tabernacle to the leader, but the leader needed the assistance of the congregation to bring it about. Moses needed an obedient and cooperative people. Scripture reveals that this was the one time the Israelites obeyed Moses without grumbling and complaining. Because the congregation was obedient and cooperated with the leader, the Tabernacle was built as God commanded.

Notice the beauty of order in the work of the Lord. The people did not carry out their assigned duties according to their own tastes, opinions, dictates or time frames, but as Moses instructed. This was good and wise because God only gave the blueprints of the master plan to one person – Moses, the leader. In this instance, the multitude of workers obeyed and respected their leader and his commands, as he obeyed and respected God and God's commands. Each tribe did what it was supposed to do, as Moses had assigned their tasks. There was no confusion or chaos. As a result, God was pleased not only with the finished product *but with the spirit in which it was finished.* This was evidenced by His manifested Shekinah Glory that filled the completed Tabernacle. Such a blessing and presence would never have occurred if Moses had not established order amongst those he led, and if those he led had not respected that order. Without order, the Israelites might never have experienced the presence, glory and blessings of God.

Perhaps that was God's purpose all along in having all of the Israelites assist in the construction and furnishing of the holy Tabernacle, rather than empowering one person or one family alone to do it. Order and unity in God's house, among God's people, is essential if His Kingdom work is to be accomplished. Take a moment and see how it applies to the presence or absence of order in your church or to your obedience to your God-appointed shepherd.

THE DESTRUCTIVENESS OF DISORDER

Now contrast the order demonstrated in Exodus to the events recorded in the Book of Judges. This book of the Old Testament gives us a very graphic picture of what happens when there is no God-ordained leader and no order among the people of God.

After the death of Joshua, the nation of Israel found itself without a leader. As a result, the people backslid into idolatry and became prey to the Canaanite enemies that surrounded them. Although He was displeased with His people, merciful God would raise up a judge to serve as a leader among the Israelites. Whenever God raised up a judge, the people were delivered from their enemies. They then repented of their idol worship, vowing to worship and serve only Jehovah, the one true God. However, this only lasted throughout the life of the judge. As soon as the judge died and the people were again without a leader, they slid back into idolatry, worshiping the false gods of the unsaved. They adopted the ways of the heathen nations that surrounded them; yet, they simultaneously and hypocritically called themselves the "blessed of the Lord."

In doing so, they not only displeased God, they stirred up His wrath. Their return to idolatry led to dire results; they either became captives and slaves to those other nations, or faced the dire threat of captivity. And yet, the God they had abandoned still had mercy on them and raised up yet another judge, who delivered them out of captivity and back to God. Of course, as soon as this judge died the people backslid again and did that which was evil in the sight of God. Once again, after captivity for some years, they were again delivered by the mercy of God through a judge He had raised up.

The entire Book of Judges describes this yo-yo pattern. Approximately 400 years of Hebrew history covered in the Book of Judges is replete with the spiritual instability and absence of holiness that plagued this chosen people who had been consecrated for Kingdom work. The Bible describes this chaos as such: *"In those days there was no king [no pastor] in Israel, but every man did that which was right **in his own eyes**."* (Emphasis added). [Judges 17:6].

No one was in charge! Everyone was in charge of himself! Everyone was doing his own thing! Utter confusion reigned. There were no rules. There was no order. And guess what else? There was no peace. There was no rest. There was no security. And there was no favor with God.

Is this what you want for your church? I pose this question to every reader, but especially to those who accuse their shepherd of having a "controlling spirit" whenever he lays down God-given rules members do not want to follow. (Keep in mind I said *God*-given rules.).

Can you imagine what your church would be like without a pastor ordained and chosen by God to establish and maintain order in your church as he leads you?

Can you imagine what your church would be like if the congregation would not allow the pastor to be the leader in fact, and not just in title?

Can you imagine what your church would be like if every congregation member did what was right "in his own eyes?"

What spiritual fruit would the church harvest if the congregation refused to cooperate with and assist their pastor in carrying out the Kingdom work God assigned to him and his church? What favor would God endow to a rebellious people?

Is every member in your local church doing what is right in his own eyes, or are they following the Divine order your pastor has received from God? Think about this as you continue to read and serve in your appointed house of God.

Chapter Six

SPIRITUAL LEVITES IN THE NEW TESTAMENT CHURCH

Many of you may argue that there is no need and no place for spiritual Levites in the New Testament Church. After all, the church building does not have to be torn down, moved and reassembled frequently, as was required of the Tabernacle. That may be true, but just as the Tabernacle was the sacred place where the presence of God would come amongst the people of Israel, the church is still the sacred house of God, where the presence of the Holy Spirit is invited to hover and move. Holy services are still conducted in the church, and the pastor needs assistance to prepare and perform the services, as did the high priest of the Hebrews. The interior and exterior of the church building, as well as the dedicated things therein and without, still have to be maintained and taken care of. The pastor should not be expected to tend to the maintenance of the church edifice and the dedicated things therein, just as the high priest was neither expected nor commanded by God to tend to the maintenance of the Tabernacle and the dedicated things therein. That was the responsibility of the Levites.

Of course, you may note that New Testament Christians are not required to bring animal sacrifices to the house of God, as were the Israelites in the Old Testament. At first glance, one may conclude that since no receipt or preparation of sacrifices is required of the New Testament believers, there is no need for a New Testament "spiritual Levite" to prepare and present the pastor with sacrifices.

But I beg to differ.

It is true that God does not require animal sacrifices from New Testament believers in Jesus Christ. But you must remember that the Levites themselves were a sacrifice offered up to God; and God gave that sacrifice back to the high priest as a gift, to assist him in the service of the Lord. (See Numbers 8:11, 19). Moreover, Jesus has always required some form of sacrifice from those who would follow Him and would be called His disciples; that sacrifice is ourselves. As He sacrificed Himself for our salvation, we, as believers, should be willing to sacrifice our carnal ways, desires, agendas and ambitions for His glory. The Apostle Paul counseled the new believers in Christ to offer themselves for a life of Christian service, as members of the body of Christ, for he said:

> [1] *I beseech you therefore, brethren, by the mercies of God, that ye present your bodies a living sacrifice, holy, acceptable unto God, which is your reasonable service.*

> [2] *And be not conformed to this world: but be ye transformed by the renewing of your mind, that ye may prove what is that good and Acceptable, and perfect, will of God.* [Romans 12: 1-2]

That reasonable service is still needed in the church, the house of God. That service is needed as "helps ministry" to the pastor, for the benefit of others, just as the service of the Levites was needed as "helps ministry" to the high priest, for the benefit of others. In sacrificing themselves as a "help's ministry" to the high priest, the Levites did far more than help prepare animal sacrifices and transport the Tabernacle from one place to another. They reached out and ministered to the people, under the direction of the high priest, for the benefit of the people.

As we get closer and closer to the end of the Age of the Church, we should be even more willing to sacrifice our time, our finances, our talents, our gifts – both spiritual and natural, our abilities, our education, our intelligence and our skills, in service to our pastor and our church, so that the "work of the ministry" can go forth. There are still many precious souls out there who want or need to receive salvation, deliverance, freedom from the captivity of demons, emotional and physical healing, and restoration to God. They need the sacrifice of our "reasonable service" in order to receive this.

The New Testament Church has to: spread the Good News (preach the gospel); proclaim that the Messiah had come; baptize believers; establish places of local assembly for believers (churches); maintain those places of assembly; teach converts the ways and commands of our Lord and Savior; minister to the poor, the needy, the defenseless and the aged; protect and defend the church, the gospel and themselves against opposition; cast out demons; and heal the sick, the afflicted and the mentally ill. The list goes on and on.

Read the New Testament for yourself and you will agree that there was much work to be done by the First Century Church. There still is. Just as it was then, so it is now. There is too much Kingdom work left to do to expect the pastors, alone, to accomplish; your service as a member of the congregation is still required. In fact, look again at some of the duties the Old Testament Levites performed, and see if you do not find yourself performing some of the same duties in your local church today:

- Set up, dismantled and transported the tent of the Tabernacle, the vessels, the instruments, and other things within the Tabernacle (SET UP TEAMS, DRIVERS AND TRANSPORTATION WORKERS);
- Received the animal sacrifices from the people and prepared them for the high priest to offer them up to God on the holy altar (MINISTERS AND ALTAR WORKERS);
- Porters, doorkeepers and gatekeepers of the gates and doors of the Tabernacle/Temple (USHERS AND GREETERS);
- Singers who sang songs of praise and worship to God, both day and night (CHOIRS AND PRAISE TEAMS);
- Musicians who played by themselves and/or accompanied the singers (MUSICIANS)
- Made the ointment and spices used in the sacred services, prepared the shewbread, and took care of the vessels used in the sanctuary (COMMUNION WORKERS AND KITCHEN STAFF);

- Offered up prayers of praise and thanksgiving and prayers of petition for the needs of the people (**PRAYER WARRIORS AND INTERCESSORS**);
- Oversaw the treasuries of the house of God (**FINANCE COMMITTEE**);
- Scribes (**DOCUMENT WRITERS for the priest**);
- Taught the Law to the people (**SUNDAY SCHOOL, CHILDRENS' CHURCH AND BIBLE CLASS TEACHERS**);
- Heard, judged and resolved controversies among the people (**COUNSELORS**);
- Warriors who protected the king (**ARMOR BEARERS AND SECURITY**).

There is a place and a Kingdom work waiting for every saved person who is a member of a church whose doors are open in the name of Jesus Christ. The works may differ from church to church and from saint to saint, but every saint in the Kingdom of God has a God-ordained work to do. Let us get busy performing our reasonable services as New Testament Levites to our shepherds.

Chapter Seven
EVERY JOINT SUPPLIETH

I think if I was ever told by God that I could preach one message to people, just one, and He let me choose the topic, I would say, "The title of my message today is: *Every Joint Supplieth: God Is Not A Respecter of Persons*".

That's it. That is what I would preach to the saints of God. I would preach it to those who have confessed Jesus as the Christ, their Lord, and the Son of the Living God. I would preach it to those who are trying to live a righteous and holy life before God and man. I would preach it to those who, in obedience to the command of God, have assembled themselves with other saints as a church whose foundation is God. I would preach it to those who truly want to serve God in the house of God.

And why would I focus on that audience and that message? I would preach that message because every saint is important to God. Unfortunately, there are saints who do not feel that every saint in their local church is important to them or to their church. Many members have left the church God planted them in because of wounds they have received by the actions, deeds and words of other members. Some have left brokenhearted; some have left in anger; some have left in bitterness. Of course, some have left because they were just looking for an excuse to leave.

Now, we know that every church has had members who left because they wanted to do their own thing, because they no longer wanted to live holy, or because they did not agree with or did not want to follow the instructions of the leadership. Sometimes those members were sent by the enemy to stir up strife, discontent and a spirit of rebellion among the congregation. When these types of members leave your church, count your blessings!

But I'm not focusing on these "aint's" right now. The particular saints I am focusing on, who I call "wounded soldiers", did not leave because they stopped loving God or His commands. They did not stop loving the people of God. They did not get tired of holiness. They did not get angry with their pastor or first lady. No, they left because their "sisters and brothers in Christ" drove them away through their hurtful actions and words. The saints spiritually murdered them. What is worse is that there are even more "wounded soldiers" who are still in their local church, silently suffering from "saint abuse."

Ephesians 4:16 states: *"From whom the whole body fitly joined together and compacted by that which every joint supplieth, according to the effectual working in the measure of every part, maketh increase of the body unto the edifying of itself in love."* The word of God declares that "every joint supplieth", making clear that every part of the body is important and has something needed by the Body of Christ. God used the analogy of various parts of the physical body to illustrate that each saved saint in local church congregations has his own unique role to fulfill to enable the whole body to function properly. (See 1 Corinthian 12:13-27). His word emphasizes that every part is needed. Of course, the head is most important because it is entrusted and equipped to provide leadership, give direction and command, promote cohesiveness throughout the body and insure that the body as a whole functions as God wills. But God did not state or imply that any remaining part of the body is more important than any other part of the body. Nor did God say that any body part has the right to denigrate the usefulness of the other parts. The congregation of your local church represents the various body parts that comprise the composite body of Christ.

Yet, many congregations have developed an attitude and class system that classifies and ranks the value of the members according to superficial factors that have no relationship to the declaration of God. Sadly, a church too often determines the importance, value and even spirituality of its members by such worldly factors as:

- Church title or appointment;
- Educational level and/or title;

- Financial stability and economic level;
- Age;
- Popularity with other members of the congregation;
- Visibility in the church;
- Relationship to the pastor or first lady;
- Relationship with the pastor or first lady.

Notice that nowhere among these shallow criteria man establishes is there mention of the individual's exemplification of true Christ-like character. There is no mention of character that reflects the nine fruit of the Spirit. There is no mention of character that reflects steadfast spiritual integrity and righteousness, or character that reflects true humility (not that faked behavior performed and exhibited in the presence of the pastor and first lady).

Sadly, those who cannot lay claim to any of those superficial, worldly factors above are too often considered to be of little importance or usefulness to Kingdom work. Consciously or unconsciously, members of their church relegate them to the outer limits of the camp, known as "the valley of the unimportant ones." Sometimes they do not even warrant a sincere and genuine "God bless you. How are you?", unless others want something from them. Barring that, they are often overlooked, maligned, neglected or simply ignored by their fellow believers.

But they are not overlooked by God.

These precious souls who man rejects, dismisses or ignores *in the church* are so very dear to God Almighty, Who created and loves them as much as the "important ones" who have cast them aside. God loves these "rejected ones" who remain faithful to God and their church in the midst of such neglect or persecution. They love God and they may know that God loves them; but God meant for congregation members to love each other and work together. Instead, "saint abuse" has wounded these souls to the point that they feel unable or unworthy to fulfill the call God has for them.

All will give account to God for their actions or inactions, both those saints who "abuse" other saints and those saints who accept the discouraging remarks and actions of their persecutors rather than rehearse the word of God to them.

Chapter Eight
SAINT ABUSE

The existence and practice of "saint abuse" in the church is not a subject most saints, church leaders, ministers and pastors want to discuss. Most do not even want to acknowledge, admit or even consider that saint abuse, as well as a "class system" may exist in their church. Please understand that when I speak of a class system in the church, I do not mean a hierarchy of authority that lines up with the word of God and the orderly structure established by the shepherd of the house. Remember, our God is a God of order and His local churches should reflect that. No, I am referring to the presumption some have that just because of who they are or because of the position they hold they are inherently a better servant of God and more "worthy" than their fellow brother or sister in Christ. In my eyes, this is just another form of saint abuse.

But if we don't cease from turning a blind eye and a deaf ear to these practices, and instead begin to stir up the courage to address them, we very well may be declared to be spiritual murderers responsible for the spiritual deaths of many who had been sanctified (set aside) for God's work. If we do not address these matters and take steps to end this abuse, we may find ourselves responsible and accountable at Judgment for the spiritual death of many whom God had intended to use for His great end-time work. We may have to answer to God for causing the spiritual abortion of that which God had planned to birth in some of His servants.

When I observe the practice of this class system and "saint abuse" toward other saints, I often wonder how our congregations would have treated many of those we read about in the Bible. We so admire the biblical servants of God, such as Moses; Joseph; Mary the mother of Jesus; Mary Magdalene; King David; Rahab; the widow of Zarapheth; and Job. But would we have accepted them with Christ-like open arms, as loved and valued members of our congregation, who had committed their lives to Christ, *before* we knew the destiny God had for them? Let us look briefly at their background reported to us in the Bible before their greatness was manifested.

Moses was a murderer; he killed a man in cold blood. He did not turn himself in to the proper authorities and confess his horrible crime. Instead, he ran away from his country, a fugitive from justice, as it were.

Joseph was not even liked or wanted by his own brothers. He held the very lowest position in the labor market – that of a slave. He was accused of being a rapist, was condemned as a felon and sentenced to prison for years.

Mary, the mother of Jesus, became pregnant while she was engaged but not yet married. To make matters worse, she did not become pregnant by the man to whom she was engaged. Even worse, she denied that she had had premarital relations with anyone, while at the same her physical condition protested otherwise. Some would have labeled her a promiscuous teenager, a liar, and a "loose" woman who bore an illegitimate child.

Mary Magdalene was said by some to be an unwilling, tormented carrier of seven demons that lived in her and controlled her. Others said she was a common prostitute.

King **D**avid – oh my goodness – was guilty of adultery with Bathsheba, another's man's wife; guilty of trying to disavow that he had impregnated Bathsheba; guilty of plotting her husband's murder; and guilty of abusing his royal position and authority to bring about the husband's murder, just so he could marry Bathsheba himself.

Rahab was not only a prostitute but a member of a people who were enemies of God's chosen people.

Widow of **Z**arapheth was poor, poorer, po'; she was well below the national poverty line. She was so poor she could not even buy food for her child. She was so poor that her plan to care for her child was to fix a last, meager meal for the two of them, and then await death. Some would have called her a bad and neglectful mother, and an endangerment to her child. They might have promptly telephoned Social Services to take the child away and press criminal charges against the mother. Others might have treated her as an outcast because she was not in the "right" economic status.

Job – oh my! Some would have insisted that he had lost the favor of God. Everything about his changed circumstances screamed REJECTED BY GOD!!! After all, he fell from great wealth in all areas to abject poverty. He fell from being the head of a model family, complete with a loving wife, seven sons and three beautiful daughters, to being childless and spiritually abandoned by his wife. He deteriorated from wondrous health to great suffering, with a seemingly incurable physical affliction that not only caused great continual pain but a horrible body odor as well. He was reduced from living in the grandest fashion to living outside the city, in the city garbage dump. He fell from being the most respected and admired citizen of his community, regarded as the most saved, righteous man among them, to being ostracized by that same community. Job fell from the Mountain of Abundance to the Valley of Abasement. He had done nothing wrong but was treated as if he had!

If these same people had gotten saved and delivered, joined your church, and desired to participate in the work of the church...before their destiny was prophesied or manifested...how would you have treated them? Remember, these were real people, not fictional characters out of someone's imagination. Just think about it. Be honest with yourself. You cannot grow in Christ and become more Christ-like if you cannot even be honest with yourself.

JOB

Let's take a closer look at the treatment brother Job received from the men who came to see him. It is difficult to label them as his "friends". They were some of the most negative people described in the Bible. Nowhere in any of their discussions did they offer a word of hope, comfort or encouragement to Job. And their conclusions about the cause of Job's plight as well as the advice they offered were so wrong! They spoke from their own limited carnal knowledge and understanding, rather than from revelatory insight from God.

While they sat with him for days before they spoke, did they ever pray for him? Did they ask God for revelation and understanding concerning Job's abased state? Did they seek God's guidance for the right words to say or actions to take on Job's behalf?

While Job's friends professed to proclaim God's judgment upon Job, they had no clue of God's true thoughts toward Job. It never entered their minds that God may have *allowed* satan to afflict Job so fiercely because God was sure of Job's love, commitment and faith toward God. They never considered that God may have been using Job as an eternal declaration that: *Jehovah has people of God whose commitment to Him will not fail, even in the midst of the most intense adversity.* These "friends" of Job never considered that God would use Job to demonstrate to man and the devil that the love some believers profess toward God is not conditioned on the degree of blessings (things) they receive from God.

Yes, Job may have cried and asked God *"Why?"* He may have had bouts of depression and moments of despair; but he never left God. He did not understand why calamity after calamity was happening to him, but he never gave up on God. At times, he may have given up on himself and He may have questioned God; but he never doubted the existence or sovereignty of God. He never followed or even considered the foolish advice of his wife to curse God. He never let the words and "counsel" of his so-called friends persuade him to give up all hope of deliverance, deny the righteousness of God or take God off the throne. I believe God chose and allowed Job to be subjected to these severe trials by the devil because God knew He could depend on Job.

It is really ironic to realize that these friends (and probably the whole community) looked down on Job and concluded that he must have lost the favor of God; yet God ascribed greatness to Job for his steadfast worship of God during this Kingdom work. Yes, this was Kingdom work: consider how the Book of Job is an evangelistic reading, encouraging us even now in the midst of our own trials and tribulations. God ultimately proved to all that Job had great, great favor with God. In fact, God was so angry with the friends because of their self-righteous criticism of Job and their presumption that they knew the mind of God, that He declared that only Job's intercessory prayers for them would avert God's wrath against them.

> *⁷And it was so, that after the Lord had spoken these words unto Job, the Lord said to Eliphaz the Tenamite, My wrath is kindled against thee, and against thy two friends: for ye have not spoken of Me the thing that is right, as My servant Job hath.*

> *⁸Therefore take unto you now seven bullocks and seven rams, and go to My servant Job and offer up for yourselves a burnt-offering; and My servant Job shall pray for you: for him will I accept: lest I deal with you after your folly, in that ye have not spoken of Me the thing which is right like My servant Job.* [Job 42: 7-8]

How are you regarding your sisters and brothers in Christ? When trials and difficulties come upon them, is it your prayers for them or your self-righteous judgments about them that are being heard by God? I'm just asking. Remember, they are a part of the same body you are joined with.

Chapter Nine
LESSONS LEARNED FROM A BASKETBALL GAME

The Holy Ghost used a high school basketball game to demonstrate to me God's Kingdom principle that "every joint supplieth."

My church has a kindergarten-through-twelfth grade private Christian school, the P.A. Owens Christian Academy. The Academy has a basketball team – the Soaring Eagles -- of which we are immensely proud. The team members have basketball uniforms, hoodies and team jackets which they wear both to identify them as Soaring Eagles and to demonstrate their unity.

But the demonstrated unity does not stop there. Many members of my church faithfully turn out in huge numbers at every one of their games to support our Soaring Eagles. Some wear the specially designed T-shirts that denote us as Soaring Eagles fans. Others wear the purple, burgundy or white knit shirts or hoodies that are part of the school uniform. We wear both outfits to signify our unity and support of the team.

We have an official cheer team, made up of some of the pre-teen and teen girls of our church and school. At certain events they lead us in cheers for the team. But we also have the "cheerleaders of the stands" who initiate cheers for our team from their seats in the bleachers. Some of the fans bring pom-poms; some bring small bullhorns; some just bring their voices to cheer loudly for our team throughout the game.

While our boys are playing hard on the court, and their coaches are intensely watching and coaching every play, we, the fans, are working just as hard in the stands to encourage them and let them know we are with them. The goal of the players, coaches and fans?—to win the game!!!

Now, this is what the Holy Ghost showed me about every joint supplying. Not every person was doing the same thing, but everyone – players, coaches and fans – were unified in striving toward the same goal. The players each had their specially assigned position on the team, based on the playing abilities and gifts God gave them. The head coach and assistant coaches had their particular duties and assignments in relation to the team, and they focused on those respective duties. No assistant coach suddenly decided that he wanted to be the head coach. The head coach did not suddenly run onto the court to shoot a free throw. And most definitely, no player decided to tell the coach what he was going to do, in opposition or rebellion to the coach's instructions. Instead, everyone knew his own responsibility and performed it to the best of his ability, for the sake of the common goal or prize – a win for the team. The coaches coached; the players played.

Likewise, none of the fans ran onto the court to replace one of the players or coaches. The fans' job was to keep the momentum going, keep the fire and passions burning in the hearts of the players, and keep them encouraged, hopeful, motivated and determined to win. It was the fans' job to drive all feelings of discouragement, defeat, despair and doubt away from the minds and hearts of their team.

Just as the team players had their different playing styles, so did the fans have their different ways of showing support. Some fans were very vocal throughout the game and cheered every time a cheer was started. Some fans stood up every time one of our players made a basket. Some fans were rather quiet, but they were praying for the team throughout the game. And some fans did very little of the above or none of the above; but they were able to encourage the team just by their presence alone. These fans consistently attended the games. One of the staunchest fans of our team was a 97-year old member of the church's Mothers Board. She was there at every game, no matter the distance she had to travel to the game site. She was there, no matter what time the game was to start. She was there from start to finish of the game, whether our team was winning or losing. The team could always depend upon her attendance at a game. And like the more outwardly, active fans, she cheered the team at the end of the game with our traditional cheer, *"WE ARE PROUD OF YOU; YES WE ARE PROUD OF YOU!'*

The Holy Ghost gave me the insight that every person who participated in the game had a task to perform, as player, coach or loyal fan. Every task and everyone who performed their respective task was needed in order to achieve the goal of winning the game, or at least, giving our all to win the game. And guess what? No one criticized anyone else; or looked down on anyone else; or denigrated anyone else; or devalued anyone else; or ostracized anyone else; or ignored anyone else; or insulted, mocked or otherwise emotionally abused anyone else for the task he or she was to carry out at the game. There was complete unity at the game. Even if the team had lost a game (which, thank God, they did not) we were still winners. How so? We were winners because fans, players and coaches from other teams saw the unity of a people aligned with the Soaring Eagles basketball team. More importantly, they saw the unity of saints and servants of our Lord and Savior Jesus Christ. There was no abuse of each other; instead, there was respect for what every joint supplied.

By the way, at the end of that 2011-2012 high school basketball season, our Soaring Eagles were undefeated and won the first place championship title and trophy in their league. And by the grace of God, with the same strategy, we won the championship the following year as well. **"WE ARE PROUD OF YOU; YES WE ARE PROUD OF YOU!"**

Chapter Ten
STOP BEING A VICTIM

"Saint abuse" may exist in your congregation. You may even have been the victim of such ill treatment. But you cannot use "saint abuse" as a convenient excuse to stop your Levitical tasks. It is no reason to leave the place where God planted you, unless God (not your carnal desires) told you to leave. It no reason to stop doing the work God called you to do. A cry of "saint abuse" is no reason to abandon your destiny. Do not, I repeat, *do not* let anyone or anything, whether human or demonic, chase you away from your place of blessing, from your destiny or from the earthly and heavenly rewards awaiting you for completing your God-ordained assignment.

You may have convinced yourself that you have justifiable reasons to leave your church. Often times, the charge of saint abuse is imagined and a cover-up for the alleged "victim's" own insecurities or immaturity. On the other hand, some of your fellow church members may, in fact, mistreat or disrespect you. Admittedly, they are wrong and will have to answer to God for that. But before you decide to throw in the towel and walk away from your church, your destiny, your Levitical assignment, and possibly from God, think about Jesus.

As I recall – and so will you – Jesus was not treated as a king by everyone, even though He was the *King of Kings*. He was not given respect and honor as a lord, even though He was the *Lord of Lords*. His own earthly brothers and sisters did not initially recognize or respect Him for who He was.

During His life on earth, Jesus was lied on, asked to leave towns, pushed out of towns, almost pushed off of a steep cliff, threatened, defamed and looked upon with suspicion, mistrust and derision, often by the same people He had helped and delivered. He endured all of this right up to the time He had to endure the false accusations, the numerous "kangaroo court" trials, the spitting, the mocking, and the unwarranted beatings by fists and flogging with whips. All of that preceded His humiliation and death by crucifixion on the cross as a common criminal. He endured all of that because of His commitment to God the Father to complete His assigned Kingdom work and because of His unconditional love for us. He had done nothing wrong to deserve this mistreatment but He endured it for the sake of others.

Because Jesus endured all of that abuse and yet finished His work, death could not hold Him. On the third day after His death, some of His female disciples discovered that His body was not in the tomb, that He had been resurrected and that He was alive, just as He had prophesied. Because He endured all of the abuse and still fulfilled His destiny, He is seated in His rightful place in Heaven, on a throne on the right hand of God the Father, wearing His holy crown as God the Son.

Because our Lord and Savior Jesus Christ did not let verbal abuse, emotional abuse, rejection and excruciating physical pain at the hands of others cause Him to disavow His Kingdom work, mankind – that includes you – was granted the opportunity to be reconciled to God the Father. Jesus became that "Open Door" through which mankind could regain the place with God he had once possessed in the Garden of Eden, before he let sin enter his heart.

And you say you cannot offer yourself and perform your Levitical services toward God, your pastor (Jesus' undershepherd) or your church because there are some in your church who do not like you or treat you right? You may want to rethink that decision. You are saved because of what Jesus was willing to endure, in spite of the ill-treatment by so-called "believers" in God. You do not know who Jesus may be trying to reach, save and deliver through you and your service in the house of the Lord.

Jesus did not fail us. We cannot fail Him. We owe God all of our service; we owe Him everything – and then some! The Bible proclaims, prophesies and promises that *"every knee shall bow and every tongue shall confess that Jesus Christ is Lord."* You will say those words of confession and Jesus will hear everyone declare His Lordship. The question is: Will you hear Him say to you, *"Well done, My good and faithful servant"*? Examine yourself carefully before you answer. Measure your response against the word of God, not your comparison to others.

The followers of Jesus had to be spiritual soldiers. Non-believing Jews, unsaved Gentiles and the Roman government persecuted the members of the first century Church. This persecution was not directed exclusively toward Peter, James, John and the other apostles. All who professed that Jesus was the Messiah, the Son of the only true God and their Lord and Savior faced this opposition. And yet, the believers persevered. And yet, they served. Whether poor or rich; whether slave or free; whether male or female; whether of high office, low office or no office; whether held in high esteem or lacking even self-esteem, they held high the banner of Christ, the gospel and holiness through their service. Their position did not matter. Position should not matter to us either. Whatever work you are called and ordained by God to do is a great work, for we serve a great God.

I once heard a radio preacher say that the first century Church was not an audience; it was an army. He was so right; he just agreed with what the word of God says. (See, for example Ephesians 6:11-17; Romans 12:13; 2 Timothy 2:3-4). You are supposed to be a soldier in the army of the Lord. You sing the songs, *"I'm A Soldier in the Army of the Lord"*, and *"Onward Christian Soldiers."* Well, sometimes soldiers get hurt, sometimes they are seriously wounded; but they don't stop fighting. They continue to fight, especially if the preservation of their lives depends on their tenacity and determination to win the battle. As a saint of God, you are in an on-going battle with satan and his demonic forces, the enemies of God. The enemy will use whatever weapon he thinks will keep you from being that soldier for Christ, including your own insecurities and weaknesses.

But you are a part of the Church, that holy and righteous force against which the gates of hell will not prevail. You have the right to call upon the power of God the Holy Ghost to help you to fight and overcome the battles that come your way. You are not only defending the glory of God and tearing down satan's kingdom; you are fighting for your soul salvation as well.

Stop being a victim. Stop crying the "baby blues." Stop expecting everyone to pamper you. Stop letting the devil pull the chains of your feelings and emotions. Are you a warrior or a wimp? Toughen up and stay the course! Finish the race!

Chapter Eleven
BE STRONG AND VERY COURAGEOUS

Just as "saint abuse" has no place among the saints of God, neither should fear and passivity find a home amongst the saints. There is a Divine command to every saint of God to be fearless in performing the Kingdom work God equips them for. You will be ineffective and of no help whatsoever to your pastor if you are too afraid to perform the ministerial assignment given to you.

Saints, the Church is in a war to reclaim or preserve those things that belong to the Kingdom of God. We have a real enemy who will stop at nothing to prevent each of us from doing our part 'to secure and safeguard the Kingdom, tear down the gates of hell, and win souls for Christ. It is the responsibility of God's people to see that our enemy does not succeed. This responsibility does not lie with your pastor alone; the lay congregation – that's you – must also do its part. Courage is required to participate in God's Kingdom work; for the Kingdom of heaven suffers violence, but the violent – the saints of God – must take and preserve it by force. (See Matthew 11:12)

One of the greatest weapons the devil uses against the people of God is fear. Make no mistake about it; there is a spirit of fear that strives to enter in and rest in the hearts of God's servants. This spirit of fear is not of God; it is from satan himself. From Genesis to Revelation the Holy Bible records God's instructions, admonitions, warnings, counsel, encouragement and enlightenment concerning the stalking presence of fear that will try to overtake us in our Christian work and journey.

Yet, our Omniscient God and Father does not leave us without an arsenal of weapons to counteract and defuse those used by the devil. *"For God has not given us the spirit of fear; but of power, and of love, and of a sound mind."* [2 Timothy 1:7]. When the spirit of fear successfully prevents us from doing what God commands, it is because we mistakenly try to perform the work and fight the devil in our own strength. However, you do not have to rely on your strength alone to contend with the devil as you fulfill your Levitical duties. Actually, it is unwise to try to contend with the devil in your own strength. You will lose. But God assured us that *"greater is He that is in you than He that is in the world."* [1 John 4:4] That "He" is God the Holy Ghost.

God will supply the strength you need. God will supply the weapons you need. God will even supply the courage you need to gain victory. He will pour courage into you, if you will let Him. God does this by encouraging you to encourage yourself. *"How will He do this?"* you ask. He will do this by reminding you of the promises He made to you, both through His written word in the Bible (the logos) and through the more personal promises He made to you specifically (the rhema word).

He will encourage you by having you rehearse the trials and difficulties you experienced in the past – you know, those situations you thought you would never survive, the ones you thought would be the end of you. God will jog your memory to reflect and remember that you did survive those hard times and, moreover, conquered some things in the process. He will remind you that not only did He give you the strength to endure during those difficult times, but that He was right there with you through it all.

Here is the caveat: You must desire to have this courage. You must ask for this courage. You must accept this courage. You must apply this courage as you carry out your spiritual, Levitical helps ministry service to God and your pastor.

When Joshua accepted the spiritual baton from Moses to lead the Israelites out of the wilderness and into the Promised Land, one of the first words God spoke to the new leader was an admonition to overcome any fear he had to carry out his assignment. Joshua 1:6-7 and 9 records God's words of encouragement:

> *⁶ Be strong and of a good courage: for unto this people shalt thou divide for an inheritance the land which I sware unto their fathers to give them.*

> *⁷ Only be strong and very courageous, that thou mayest observe to do according to all the law, which Moses My servant commanded thee: turn not from it to the right hand or to the left, that thou mayest prosper whithersoever thou goest.*

> *⁹ Have not I commanded thee? Be strong and of a good courage; be not afraid, neither be thou dismayed: for the Lord thy God is with thee withersoever thou goest.*

Now, let's stop, examine these verses and think about this for a moment. For almost forty years, Joshua had seen what Moses had to contend with as he led upward of three million complaining, never-satisfied ex-slaves through the wilderness. He saw the wondrous miracles God had performed through Moses. He witnessed God's answer to Moses' prayers for the people. He also saw the frustration and anger Moses felt and sometimes displayed because of the fickleness and unbelief of the people. Moreover, Joshua knew that Moses failed to enter the Promised Land because he let the people and the pressure of their complaints get to him: Moses became impatient and presumptuous as a result of his frustration and missed giving God the glory for providing water out of a rock.

Then, God gave Joshua the task of picking up where Moses left off! Joshua had to take the second generation of freed slaves into hostile territory, command them to take it from the warlike people who had been occupying those territories for years and years, and then take possession of it as their own! Joshua had to be a warrior-general and leader of this new nation called Israel as it went forth to confront and defeat thirty-one enemy kings … on the enemy's own turf, the land God had promised to Israel.

Joshua had to achieve this monumental task without a blueprint or a prepared strategy. He had to do this with a people who were not warriors by nature, or an army by nature, or a fighting people by nature. (Remember, they were former slaves who had not even been permitted to look their masters eyeball to eyeball, much less fight against them).

Do you think that maybe, just maybe, Joshua had reason to be in need of more courage than he could muster on his own? Do you think that may have been the reason God had to encourage His servant not to fear what he was charged to do? God was mindful that a spirit of fear might attack Joshua. So, before satan could effectively launch his attack, God fortified Joshua with an admonition to be strong and very courageous, and remember that the God of Moses was also with him.

Any time the will of God is to be performed by His servants, the adversary will attempt to impede its completion. The devil knows he cannot stop God, so he tries to stop the ones God chooses to use. The enemy of God will attempt to strike such fear in the saint of God that it paralyzes the believer from obeying God. Yet, we serve an all-powerful God, who gives us the strength and power to overcome any obstacle the devil lays in our paths. We can and must complete the work God has set before us. Cast out that fear and send it back to the devil! Let him be the one who fears. *"And the gates of hell shall not prevail against the church!"* [Matthew 16:18]

Chapter Twelve
YOU MUST DO YOUR PART

You have a holy Kingdom work to do for the glory of God, as did the Levites of the Old Testament and the first century Christians who were "spiritual Levites" in the New Testament. The Old Testament records that the descendents of Levi were called to provide supportive service to the high priest. The New Testament records that Peter, as head of the Church, was guided by the Holy Ghost to name other believers to "wait on tables" and offer supportive assistance, in order to free the apostles to attend to the higher spiritual matters of their office. (See Acts 6:2)

Being a Christian was never meant to be a passive experience. The New International Version of Acts 6:1-4 explains it thusly:

> *¹ In those days, when the number of disciples was increasing, the Grecian Jews among them complained against the Hebraic Jews because their widows were being overlooked in the daily distribution of food.*
>
> *²So the Twelve gathered all the disciples together and said "It would not be right for us to neglect the ministry of the Word of God in order to wait on tables.*
>
> *³Brothers, choose seven men from among you who are known to be full of the Spirit and wisdom. We will turn this responsibility over to them.*

> *⁴ And will give our attention to prayer and the ministry of the word."*

Even before Jesus completed His earthly ministry and ascended back to Heaven, He prepared others to continue His work. In doing so, He did not limit the preparation and the work to the twelve apostles.

> *¹After these things the Lord appointed other seventy also, and sent them two and two before His face into every city and place, whither He Himself would come.*
>
> *²Therefore said He unto them, The harvest truly is great, but the labourers are few: pray ye therefore the Lord of the harvest, that He would send forth labourers into His harvest*
>
> *¹⁹Behold, I give you power to tread on serpents and scorpions and over all the power of the enemy.* [Luke 10:1-2, 19]

The Christian life is a very active and selfless life, devoted to both obeying the will of God and glorifying His name, the reward of which is an eternal, blissful life with Him. God does not give us gifts, callings and anointings just so they can remain dormant and ineffective for the rest of our saved lives. They are given to us for use in His Kingdom work.

Contrary to what the laity believes, and contrary to the way some may conduct their lives, you do not have to be a licensed and ordained "minister" to perform service for the Lord. The definition of "minister" is "servant". All believers in Jesus Christ are supposed to be servants of this Most High God. You cannot use the lack of ordination to the clergy as an excuse for failing to do the work God equipped you to do, or for failing to provide the help and support your pastor needs from you.

Not all of the Levites were priests, and yet they were all chosen by God to minister to (serve) the high priest and the people in various capacities. You have the same obligation. Just as God chose the Levites for the work He needed to have performed, He chose you for the work you are to do. Having chosen you, God has equipped you to serve in His house, for His glory. You did not and do not tell God what work you have *selected* to do, as if you are doing God a favor. God does the assigning through your pastor.

Your level of obedience and your willingness or lack thereof to accept and carry out the assignment and responsibilities given to you convey to God your true attitude about serving God, your pastor and your local church.

When you confessed Jesus as the Son of the Living God and professed Him to be your Lord and Savior, did you not also declare that you would serve Him? Then do it! And do it with gladness and thanksgiving. After all, Jesus voluntarily made a great sacrifice of service for us.

Jesus left His place in glory and descended from Heaven to become a human being...for us. He allowed Himself to be called out of His holy and royal name – called a son of Beelzebub ---notwithstanding that He cast out demons, the minions of the devil known as Beelzebub...for us. He allowed Himself to be arrested on false charges, lied upon, humiliated, spat upon, beaten and ultimately crucified publicly as a common criminal. He was fully aware that He could have called for a legion of angels to come to His rescue, but He refused to do so...for our salvation.

He never complained that the work He was to do was too much to ask of Him. He never said the task ahead and the opposition He would face was too frightening for Him to confront. Yes, He sought His Father, during His agony in the Garden of Gethsemane, asking first that God would remove the cup awaiting Him, and then, having acknowledged God's will, praying for the strength to fulfill His destiny. But Jesus never told God the Father *"No"*. Even when He petitioned the Father to take away the cruel cup of crucifixion and even crueler separation from the Father, Jesus never even considered making the choice to disobey the will of God the Father. Instead, in the midst of His agony, Jesus said, *"Nevertheless, not My will but Thine, be done"* [Luke 22:42]. He did all of that although He never carried the title of "priest."

He owed a debt to no one, least of all to any of us. We owe Him everything. How dare we say we cannot perform and complete our assigned Kingdom work because we are only members of the church, part of the congregation, and not an ordained minister? Away with that excuse!

The great majority of the Levites did not have the title of "high priest" or even "priest", and yet the service they were to render to the high priest, the priests and the people was just as important to God, just as "ordained" as that belonging to the titled Levitical priests. The same can be said for the seventy disciples Jesus chose and sent out to do a work in His name.

(See Luke 10:1-17) The Bible does not state that they carried the title of apostles, prophets, pastors, teachers or evangelists. There is no indication that they had any title other than *"disciples of Christ"* and *"labourers"* of the house of God. At Judgment, those same Levites and seventy disciples will be accountable to God for the service they did or did not perform, as well as the heart with which they performed their services. So will you.

Now, that does not mean that you are free to go out and "do your own ministry thing" as a representative of your local church, without direction, instruction and permission, or release from the shepherd of your church. The Levites did not decide which rotation of service they would appear for or which duties they would perform. They carried out the duties assigned to them by the high priest according to the rotation established by the high priest. Remember, God is a God of order and His house of prayer should be likewise. Moreover, the Word of God is replete with wisdom, counsel and command regarding holy authority. Do not try to force the exercise of your gift upon your pastor or your church, and, by all means, do not try to get ahead of God. As the Word of God says, your gift will make room for you (Proverbs 18:16)...with or without a title.

You do not need a title to glorify God through your service in the house of God. You just need to love Him and trust Him enough to obey Him. You just need to love Him with all your heart, your mind, your soul and your strength. You just need to remember that as a member of your congregation you are more than a *permanent benchwarmer.*

GIDEON'S ARMY

Think about the men who followed Gideon and stood with him as he obeyed God's command. They certainly didn't sit by idly, waiting for the enemy to overtake them.

I love the Old Testament story of Gideon and his 300. I love all of God's written word, but there are certain passages and stories that are particularly special to me. The story of Gideon and his 300 is one of them. Every verse of Judges 6:11 through Judges 7:23 ministers to me and inspires me as I serve in a great house of God. In their spiritual admonitions to their congregations, many pastors have frequently referred to these verses and the blossoming courage and character of Gideon. I want to focus on the 300 men that followed Gideon into battle.

We all know the story. Originally, 32,000 men signed up to fight by Gideon's side against a host of Midianites whose numbers were so great they could not be counted. We know that 22,000 of Gideon's men abandoned the quest even before the battle began, because they were afraid. Then, out of the remaining 10,000, only 300 were chosen by God to stay by Gideon's side and enter the fray. God used Gideon and these 300 to rout and defeat the Midianites.

The preached word often examines the feelings, emotions, courage and faith in God Gideon experienced, seeing 31,700 men just up and desert him before the battle began, leaving a measly 300 unarmed men to face a fierce multitude of trained, armed warriors. But consider this: Gideon was not the only person who saw this mass desertion; those 300 men also saw their numbers dwindle down from 32,000 to 300. Just like Gideon, those 300 men looked out onto the battlefield and saw the thousands of enemy soldiers they were up against. Just like Gideon, those 300 men had to have faith that God would be with them and would give them victory in a seemingly hopeless situation.

The 300 could not ride on Gideon's faith. They had to rely on their *own* faith in God. When the arrows, swords and spears were aimed toward them (or whatever weaponry the enemy was using); when the Midianites started charging Gideon's foot soldiers on camels too numerous to count, those 300 could not seek out and hide behind Gideon's faith, in hopes of surviving. Oh no, it was the exercise of their *own*, individual faith in God that strengthened them and encouraged them to stand and fight in the face of the onslaught. The level of their own faith in God reflected the level of their trust in God and the level of their belief that God was with them to defeat their formidable foe.

They could consider that Gideon's faith enabled him to lead them into battle. They could follow suit by patterning themselves after Gideon and placing their faith in the same God. Gideon's faith could serve as an example and the match by which a fire of faith could be ignited throughout the camp and hearts of the 300. But the 300 could not claim Gideon's faith as their own. They had to exercise their own faith. *Faith in God, throughout a believer's life, requires individual effort, growth and practice.*

Here is something else to think about: Gideon expected each of those 300 men who remained with him to have faith in God. Nowhere does Scripture state or infer that during the battle Gideon raced back and forth through his troops asking, *"Are you OK? Do I need to hold your hand? Do I need to pamper you?"* In fact, once Gideon told his fighting men what God had promised (victory), the weapons they would use to attain victory (lamps and trumpets!), and gave them positions (three groups of 100 each) to fight thousands of warriors, Gideon never looked back. And the men never questioned him!!! Now that took faith!

This was not only a display of faith in God, but faith in their leader, Gideon, for they were assured that Gideon would only lead them as God directed him. That was a testimony of Gideon's character and *proven* integrity among his people. It was also a testimony of their confidence in him. (But... this was all predicated on the 300 being able to follow their leader because their leader was following God. Never forget that. The entire content of this book is grounded on the mandate that you must have a God-fearing, God-ordained, holy and obedient pastor leading you as he, himself, follows the commands of God!)

I absolutely love the story of Gideon and his army of 300. It is such a beautiful display of faith-filled followers of a faith-filled leader. What a win-win combination for the glory of God! It is that beautifully balanced coin that pleases God and gets the Kingdom work completed: holy leader and holy followers. Spiritual Levites to God's chosen pastors, following and helping their leader as he follows God.

Chapter Thirteen
SELFISHNESS vs. SELFLESSNESS

We cannot be selfish with our salvation. We cannot praise, worship and thank Jesus our Lord for the unselfish sacrifice He made and the gift of salvation He offered us...which we accepted...only to sit on our salvation and hoard it for ourselves. Not everyone will be saved, not everyone will accept the offer of salvation; but we who are saved have, at the very least, a responsibility to be a witness of this same gift of salvation to as many as we can. *Every* saved Christian bears this responsibility. Title is unimportant.

When you professed to be a Christian you lost whatever right you thought you had to be selfish. When you confessed your sins, repented of them, turned your life over to Christ, confessed and professed that Jesus is the Son of the Living God and Lord of your life, you, in essence, declared that you were voluntarily becoming a Christian. In other words, you agreed that your life was to become a spiritual and natural conversion, one that would be Christ-like, reflecting the character and attributes of Christ. *Jesus was not selfish.*

There was a time when Jesus saw a great multitude of people who had followed him to a desert place. Scripture says Jesus *"was moved with compassion toward them, and He healed their sick."* [Matthew14:14]. Consider the time and unselfish love Jesus gave as He perhaps spoke a corporate word or walked through the multitude laying hands on hundreds, and perhaps thousands, allowing His healing virtue to flow from Him into their afflicted bodies and minds. They were not His relatives; they were not his BFFs (Best Friend Forever). From a natural point of view, He did not even know their names. None of that was important to Him. What was pressing on His heart was their need.

The Bible says Jesus ministered healing to the multitude into the evening, the number of which by this time reached 5,000 men, plus women and children. Notwithstanding the long day and the lateness of the day, the people would not leave, even though they had been there all day, had not eaten and had not brought much food, if any. They did not want to separate themselves from the presence of Jesus and the healing miracles He was performing. Jesus knew this. He told His disciples, *"They need not depart; give ye them to eat."* This is the account of the miraculous feeding of the 5,000-plus multitude. (See Matthew 14:15-21).

We always focus on the number of people who were fed and the fact that the fishes and loaves were multiplied so that everyone was fed. But the Holy Ghost revealed to me new insight into this miracle, which bolsters the command for unselfishness by Christians. Matthew 14:19 says, *"And He commanded the multitude to sit down on the grass, and took the five loaves, and the two fishes, and looking up to heaven, He blessed and brake, and gave the loaves to His disciples, and the disciples to the multitude."* Let me share with you what the Holy Ghost showed me.

It was Jesus who caused the food to multiply so that there was enough for everyone; but it was the disciples who distributed the food. *"He...gave the loaves to His disciples and the disciples to the multitude."* Jesus gave the food to the disciples and the disciples gave the food to the multitude. Jesus did not serve the people Himself; He commanded His disciples to feed the people. If the disciples had not given the food to the people, they would have continued to be hungry, lacking and unaware of that which Jesus had provided for them.

Again, the verse reads, *"He...gave the loaves to His disciples and the disciples to the multitude."* The Holy Ghost further opened my spiritual eyes to read the words and see that Jesus gave the food to the disciples, but He also gave the disciples *themselves* to the multitude. In other words, two entrees were provided for the hungry multitude by Jesus – the natural food of fish and loaves, and the service of the disciples themselves as ambassadors and servants of Jesus. The natural food would satisfy their physical hunger; the love of Christ for the people, reflected by the service of His disciples to the people, would satisfy their spiritual hunger.

As a New Testament Levite, you can pattern unselfish service to God and your pastor, for the sake of souls and for the glory of God, in the same spirit the disciples served their shepherd Jesus, for the sake of souls and for the glory of God. Prayerfully, through the power, authority and anointing of God, your shepherd is providing you with the word of God, the revelation of God, the blessedness of salvation from sin, and the beauty of a life of holiness and Christ-like service. Prayerfully, for the sake of your eternal soul, he is also preaching that two options are offered by God to everyone who is ever born: (1) either eternal life and bliss with the Lord in Heaven or (2) eternal torment and damnation in Hell.

Assuming that your pastor is a true and holy servant of God, you have been given soul-sustaining food through the preached word Jesus provided and gave to him. You, in turn, as a servant of God and a spiritual Levite to your pastor, are to distribute this food to those who are hungry and in need of the same. If we do not witness to the unsaved and the backslidden when commanded to by God, we may find ourselves accountable for their unfulfilled spiritual hunger and need…and our failure to offer them the option of eternal life in bliss with the Lord. Not everyone will initially come to the house of God to learn of:

1) the offer of soul salvation from sin;
2) deliverance from the possession and oppression of demonic spirits operating in their lives;
3) the power of faith in God, or;
4) the many other blessed benefits of living a life of holiness.

Rather, they will initially learn of these things through your personal testimony and the witness of your life in your daily activities. You can satisfy their initial hunger so that they will want more of Jesus. As a member of the congregation, we do not have the spiritual authority, power and anointing given to our shepherd; but my pastor and first lady have often told our congregation that our job is to witness to people and get them to the church, where they can receive from the appointed shepherds more of what God offers them. Get them to the church; God and your pastors can do the things you may not have been anointed or given spiritual authority to do. Still, we must do our part. Souls are depending on us to be unselfish. Our pastors are depending on us to be unselfish. God is depending on us to be unselfish.

"Freely ye have received; freely give." [Matthew 10:8].

Chapter Fourteen
TIME FOR A RELATIONSHIP CHECK-UP

YOUR RELATIONSHIP WITH GOD

You cannot serve God without having a personal relationship with God. You may be able to serve man without a relationship with God, but to serve *God* there has to be a relationship with Him. No matter how many ministries or auxiliaries you are a part of; no matter how many titles you wear in your church; no matter how many positions you may hold, you cannot really serve God to the uttermost unless you have a relationship with Him. You may be ever so faithful...to man. You may be sincere in your service...to man. You may get accolade heaped upon accolade from the pastor, first lady and the entire congregation for the work you do in the church and for the church. But if you do not have a personal, on-going relationship with our Lord and Savior Jesus Christ, you may be a Martha rather than a Mary in the house of God.

Now, don't get me wrong; Martha respected Jesus and acknowledged that He was Lord. She performed good works; works necessary to keep her house in order and presentable for hospitality to others. That was very important, especially because the tradition and culture of the Middle East was to readily provide hospitality, even to unexpected visitors; how much more so if that visitor was the Lord himself. Because Martha worked and cooked and cleaned, the home was presentable for the presence of God. But she was so busy with her housekeeping and cooking that she gave priority to these tasks, placing them above the opportunity to enjoy the presence of the Lord while He was in her midst. [See Luke 10:38-42] After all, Jesus did not live with Martha, Mary and their brother Lazarus. Maratha may have missed her time of visitation from the Lord.

But Mary had the better part. Mary had the best part. Jesus said so.

⁴¹And Jesus answered and said unto her, Martha, Martha, thou art careful and troubled about many things:

⁴²But one thing is needful: and Mary hath chosen that good part, which shall not be taken away from her. [Luke 10: 41-42]

Martha had approached Jesus, not to sit at His feet as Mary did, but to have Jesus rebuke Mary for not assisting her with the housework. Mary, on the other hand, nurtured and coveted a personal relationship with Jesus above all else. She intuitively understood that having Jesus in her physical presence was far more important than making sure the bread did not burn. Sitting at the feet of Jesus, while He blessed them with His presence, gave sense to everything she would do thereafter. Remember, it is believed by many that it was this same Mary who washed Jesus' feet with her tears of worship and thanksgiving, anointed His feet with her expensive perfumed oil, and then dried them with her hair. Jesus was so touched by her choice to value her relationship with Him above all else that He used it as a lesson to others. It is still a lesson to us today. Do you know you can serve faithfully in your house of worship...with the presence of God in the church...and still miss God? How sad is that?

So, what am I saying? Am I saying that you should never do physical work in and for the house of God? You should never sweep a floor, pick up a piece of paper, move some tables, clean a toilet, wash some dishes, clean the sanctuary, usher, sing in the choir, work security, or drive the church bus to pick up members and visitors, even if your service would lighten your pastor's load? No, by all means, no! The work is necessary and must be done to carry out and keep the physical and ministerial necessities of the house of God in order. I am saying that to be purely a "Martha" – being concerned only with the church work you are doing and the auxiliaries you are on – is no replacement for a personal relationship with Christ.

The optimal attitude and stance to have is to be both a Mary and a Martha. Both are necessary. Because Martha worked, cooked and cleaned, the home was presentable for the presence of God to enter. Everything was in order. And because Mary sat at the feet of Jesus, she not only enjoyed His presence but received something eternal, something that could not be taken from her. Even as you serve, carrying out your respective duties and necessary responsibilities in the house of God, keep the presence of Jesus foremost in your heart and spirit. Do your ministerial service – yes – but do it as unto the Lord, for His glory. Don't get so involved and busy with your church work that you have no time for a personal relationship with Jesus.

Your Relationship with the Pastorate

A personal relationship with the Lord necessarily requires that you have the right relationship with your pastor and your first lady. I'm going to say that again, in many different versions, so that we are all on the same page. You can't say you love God and have a personal relationship with Him if you hate your pastor and first lady. You can't say you love God and have a personal relationship with Him if you love your pastor but hate your first lady, who is your pastor's wife and his helpmeet. You can't say you love God and have a personal relationship with Him if you love your first lady, but you hate your pastor. As saints of God, we are not supposed to hate anything except that which God hates.

When I refer to "hatred" toward the pastorate, I include: real hatred toward them; rebellion toward their instructions, including a "goat spirit" by which you buck against everything they say or do; willful disregard for the God-given rules of the church they have established; disrespect for them personally; or disrespect for their ministerial office. Dispersed throughout this book, and underlying the whole purpose of this book, is the rooted Biblical foundation that pastors were given to the church by God, out of the love of God. Pastors were given to the local churches as undershepherds of Jesus Christ, the Chief Shepherd of the universal Church. *If* God ordained your pastor to be the shepherd of your church;

if your pastor is yet living a holy and righteous life that is pleasing to God, both in his personal life and as shepherd of the flock given him; then he is one that God spoke of when He said: *"And I will give you pastors according to Mine heart..."* [Jeremiah 3:15] and *"Obey them that have the rule over you, and submit yourselves: for they watch for your souls..."* [Hebrews 13:17]

Granted, those are crucial *"ifs"* your pastor must satisfy; but if he does, you are obligated to have a right relationship with him. We have already discussed this. We are to follow the pastor as he follows Christ. We are to be a joy and not a grief for the pastor to shepherd. As New Testament spiritual Levites, we are to be the "helps ministry" to the pastor, as God commanded us to be. You cannot be of any "help" nor can you righteously "minister to" or "serve" the pastor if you do not love and respect him. Who wants help from someone who does not even respect them?

If you think your pastor has made a mistake in judgment or with a decision he has made or plans to implement – pray about it! Covering your shepherd in prayer is your basic reasonable service. Seek the Lord's counsel. If your pastor gives you "invitation" to speak to him about the matter, and *if it is the will of God for you to do so*, do so with the utmost respect. Throughout your discussion with the pastor, and no matter what the outcome, remember that *he is the pastor; you are not*!

Pastors are earthen vessels, just as we are. They can make mistakes. (I am not talking about a willful decision to continually engage in blatant sin.) They are not Jesus, so don't expect or require that they never make a mistake in the government of the church. It is unfair to them and unrealistic for you to require that they be perfect, when they have the monumental task of shepherding a congregation made up of your imperfect self and other imperfect people. But if they err in judgment, God will counsel or correct them. Your pastor is a man of God, not a "man of the congregation." As a member of the congregation, it is not our place to try to pastor the pastor. You just continue to pray and serve well, unless and until God tells you otherwise. (And make sure you are hearing the voice of God, not your voice, your buddy's voice, or the devil's voice).

Your Relationship with Other Members

Lastly, to be an effectual spiritual Levite to your pastor, you must have a right relationship with your sisters and brothers in Christ, who are also trying to be good spiritual Levites. There are many scriptures admonishing and even commanding the saints to especially love their sisters and brothers in Christ. What scriptures require this, you ask? My response is, "Read the entire New Testament!" This command to love is not limited to you loving the members of your local congregation, exclusively; but the love should start there. The love for fellow Christians must start there. The love for mankind must start there. The members of your local congregation are the people you get to know personally; the ones you regularly worship and praise God with; the ones you take Holy Communion with; the ones you sit next to and with whom you work and serve in the church.

If you desire to have peace in your church; if you desire to have order and not confusion or chaos in your church; if you desire to truly be a spiritual Levite to your pastor; if you desire to be a joy and not grief to your shepherd as he watches for the souls of all of the congregation; if you desire for your church to maintain an effective ministry for the salvation of souls and the glory of God; if you desire to invite and enjoy the presence and power of God in your church; if you truly love God, you must strive at all times to love your brothers and sisters in Christ.

Is that easy? Not always. Some members are harder to love than others. Sometimes you, yourself, are harder to love than others…some of the time or all of the time. But the greatest weapon we have against the attacks and traps of the devil is to love with the love of God. The devil has nothing with which to combat the Church when the Church loves. The devil cannot destroy you, your pastor, the vision, or the ministry given to your local church when there is Godly love among the pastor and the members of the congregation. God will be glorified by your love.

This is truly a work in progress for all of us, pastors and Levites alike; it will be so until we stand before the throne of God. We will be judged not only on how we served, but how we loved.

> *²⁰ If a man say, I love God, and hateth his brother, he is a liar: for he that loveth not his brother who he hath seen, how can he love God whom he hath not seen?*
>
> *²¹ And this commandment have we from Him, That he who loveth God love his brother also.* [I John 4: 20-21]

Godly love – coursing from breast to breast and heart to heart among the congregation – is a shield and buckler for the church entity. Godly love – streaming down from Heaven, through the pastorate, to the congregation, and then returned upward by the same path – is a wall of defense which cannot be breached by the attacks of the devil. Godly love – that love so beautifully described in 1 Corinthians 13:1-8 – is the greatest weapon saints of God and His Church have against satan.

Don't let yourself be the one to defile the flow of God's pure love and cause a breach in the wall for the enemy to enter.

There is really nothing more I should have to say concerning this matter. Any further conversation on this particular subject must be between God and yourself. We all need much more perfecting in this area of our Christian walk and service.

Chapter Fifteen
SPIRITUAL LEVITES FITLY JOINED TOGETHER

When I think of a New Testament church congregation working together as spiritual Levites to their pastor, I envision members who are fitly joined together. This is what I mean by "fitly joined together":

Fitly: Every member performing his best in the work best suitable for him, as part of a team called the congregation, so that the work of the church can be completed.

Joined: A congregation bonded together with their pastor and each other by a belief in the same goal or vision.

Together: A congregation acting as one, to be a help to their pastor, for the glory of God.

When a congregation does not work together with the pastor and each other to accomplish a work or vision given by God to their church, the result is a nightmare called "confusion". But God is not the author of confusion; and in these end times a Christian people commanded to do a work for God cannot afford to have confusion in their midst.

The Bible says, "Where there is no vision, the *people* perish...." [Proverbs 29:18]. But, even if a church has a vision, unless the people work together as one, the *vision* may perish...at least for those people. In other words, the people may miss their destiny. Hopefully, your pastor is leading your congregation according to the ministerial mandate given by God to him for your particular church. As a member of your church congregation, your individual destiny may be wrapped up in your willingness to assist your pastor to fulfill that mandate with the same dedication, commitment and calling as was expected of the Levites of the Old Testament. Your failure to do so as part of the corporate body could cost you dearly. This is why a congregation fitly joined together is so essential.

When I think of Biblical examples of effective teamwork, I readily think of the rebuilding of the city and walls of Jerusalem, under the leadership of Nehemiah. [See the Book of Nehemiah]. Various entire families were delegated to repair or rebuild specific gates, homes and sections of the city. Craftsmen were given special construction projects that called for their unique knowledge and expertise, while others were assigned other duties, such as carrying supplies or cleaning up debris around their assigned area. Regardless of the assignment, all performed their tasks in the face of opposition. When Sanballat and Tobiah sought to hinder the work, Nehemiah instructed certain families to guard various areas of the city with swords, bows and spears, just to protect the others as they continued their work. (See Nehemiah 4:13, 21)

Nehemiah faced a great challenge in rebuilding the city and walls of Jerusalem; but because the people worked together, with the leader and each other, the work was completed according to God's plan, in the spirit that was pleasing to God. *"The people had a mind to work"* [Nehemiah 4:6] and they were "fitly joined together."

If the people were able serve and assist Nehemiah accomplish the task given him, so can we, as New Testament Levites, serve and assist our pastors to accomplish the ministry tasks given to them, by the grace, power and anointing of Christ Jesus, the Chief Shepherd.

[10] For we are His workmanship, created in Christ Jesus unto good works, which God hath before ordained that we should walk in them. [Ephesians 2:10]

[16] From whom the whole body fitly joined together and compacted by that which every joint supplieth, according to

the effectual working in the measure of every part, maketh increase of the body unto the edifying of itself in love. [Ephesians 4:16]

[19] Now therefore ye are no more strangers and foreigners, but fellowcitizens with the saints, and of the household of God:

[20] And are built upon the foundation of the apostles and prophets, Jesus Christ Himself being the Chief corner stone;

[21] In whom all the building fitly framed together groweth unto an holy temple in the Lord:

[22] In whom ye also are builded together for an habitation of God through the Spirit. [Ephesians 2: 19-22]

Chapter Sixteen
CLOSING THOUGHTS: A NOTE TO THE MEMBERS OF MY CHURCH

Saints, you see and admire the unshakeable faith our Bishop and Elect Lady have in God the Father, God the Son and God the Holy Ghost. You have been witness to and beneficiary of their tireless labor in the work of the Lord Jesus Christ. You have experienced and benefitted from their unconditional love for you, personally and corporately. You have seen with your own eyes their uncompromising determination to obey God and follow our Lord Jesus Christ, as shepherds of our church. From them you learn how to walk in and increase your faith in God. From them you learn how to serve in the house of the Lord with gladness, knowing what a privilege it is to be called into His service in any capacity. But you cannot ride on their faith alone and their service alone and expect to fulfill your own destiny and please God.

The end-time vision our church has been entrusted with is a corporate work that demands individual commitment. Each of you who was placed here by God to be a part of this vision has a work to do. Through the preached rhema words of His prophets, God has already made it clear to you that what we need to accomplish the vision is already in you. You just have to believe and trust God and His prophets, our leaders.

Gideon's army was both a single corporate unit and 300 unique individuals who faced and defeated the enemy. So are we. We carry out the vision given our church as a corporate body. And yet, this corporate body is composed of individuals who must *individually* make the commitment to:

- Live holy and give God the glory at all times;
- Have faith, belief and trust in God at all times;
- Hunger for the presence of God in your personal, daily walk, as well as among the corporate body;
- Consistently seek a closer relationship with God;
- Embrace the vision of this house;
- Remain loyal, obedient and submitted to the leadership of this house, following them as they follow Christ; and above all,
- Love God, have no other god before Him, do His will, love His chosen shepherds who watch for your eternal soul, and love His people (our sisters and brothers in Christ).

No one can do this for you. The great revelation is – YOU CAN DO IT! Believe, believe, believe! Believe the word, report and promises of God. *"Believe in God and so shall ye be established. Believe His prophets and so shall ye prosper."* [2 Chronicles 20:20].

> [23] *And whatsoever ye do, do it heartily, as to the Lord, and not unto men;*
>
> [24] *Knowing that of the Lord ye shall receive of the inheritance: for ye serve the Lord Christ.* [Colossians 3:23, 24]

NOTES

Printed in the United States
By Bookmasters